THIS IS *Sailing*
A Complete Course

illustrator **Peter A.G. Milne**

THIS IS Sailing

A Complete Course

RICHARD CREAGH-OSBORNE

second edition revised by
Steve Sleight

Hearst
Marine
Books
New York

Library of Congress Catalog Card Number: 84-62460

ISBN 0-688-05429-3

Printed in Italy

Second U.S. Edition

1 2 3 4 5 6 7 8 9 10

THIS IS Sailing
A Complete Course
RICHARD CREAGH-OSBORNE

An illustrated instructional course in small boat sailing in three parts

Preface

This book has been made to span international boundaries. This requirement raises problems of local usage and language which are occasionally insoluble but will, we hope, prove to be of minor significance when compared to the value of having a fully-illustrated sailing course.

The way a boat sails and the way to sail a boat are the same everywhere. The author and artist working together have shown in this book not only how to manage a small boat but have also conveyed the *feeling* of sailing.

With the use of colour techniques we have encouraged sailors to visualize mentally the invisible air-flow because the understanding of this is the secret of sailing. Once air-flow and its effects can be seen in the mind then all else comes clear.

The way this book has been planned may seem a little unusual but we think it is logical. The intention is for each part to be read as a whole—thus Part One will be read first to obtain a picture of the boat and how it works. The first seventeen pages form a general introduction to boats and sailing and contain brief hints of ideas which are important and which will come clear to the reader later in the course.

For example, the idea of the centreboard is introduced as early as page 4 and its mechanical operation is explained on page 26 but the real practical use of the centreboard is mentioned in a number of places and explained more fully in Part Two. But by this time it should be a familiar part of the reader's knowledge of a boat. It is no longer a new idea and its uses are already broadly understood.

Thus we have followed in the main a 'concentric' method of teaching whereby ideas are developed and expanded only as and when they are needed in the overall programme of learning to sail.

Again, the problem of apparent wind which appears to confuse so many learners, and to obsess so many teachers, has scarcely been touched upon even in Part Two except in a purely natural and practical way. A boat can be sailed quite well without the crew being aware of the theory of apparent wind and so it is only in Part Three where sudden increases in boat or wind speed are discussed that we even attempt to explain how this affects the wind as felt on board.

This course is above all a practical one. Theory has been kept to the absolute minimum and is dealt with in a graphic way with a short text to complete the explanation. In some cases purists might question some statements as being not the whole truth. However too much detail even if strictly correct, can confuse more often than it clarifies, and so we have taken a few liberties in order to get people afloat and in control of their boats as fast and safely as possible. The finer points of theory can follow later.

Finally, at whom are we aiming this course? Sailing is so wide a subject and covers such different types of craft which can be sailed by people of all ages, that there is a danger of dealing with too great a range of subjects too thinly. Therefore we have concentrated here on the type of modern light centreboard boat which would appeal to the thousands of people who want to enjoy an exciting and relaxing sport. Once control of a light dinghy is mastered it will be easy to transfer to any other type of boat and the interplay of forces which make a boat sail will be fully understood.

One Introduction to a Boat

The beginnings of hull design

The design of boats gradually evolved in several separate streams of development according to the materials and skills available locally. Thus, the coracle was made from local skins and laths; the box-like river ferry was an improved log-raft made from roughly shaped planks with built-up sides to increase capacity; and the canoe was refined from the earliest hewn-out tree trunks.

A square sided box has the greatest possible carrying capacity and is still used today in only slightly modified form for ferrying animals, goods and vehicles across rivers by means of ropes or cables or, in certain cases, propelled by poles.

In all except dead smooth water the box-raft has grave disadvantages. Not only do waves splash inboard too easily, but free water or loose goods inside cause extreme instability, which is difficult to correct. The craft also has little directional stability and is hard to keep straight as well as it being nearly impossible to alter course without excessive sideslip.

Quite another line of development produced the coracle, built with great economy of material. Skins stretched over a lath framework show the beginnings of a built-up system of construction which has lasted for thousands of years and is only now being superseded for larger and larger craft by various forms of moulding techniques.

The coracle was a good weight carrier and its shape was a great improvement for seaworthiness. However it was still hard to control, tending to spin when pushed with a pole and being excessively tiring to pull along with a paddle.

Different again were the long thin canoes which started as being single logs hollowed out by fire or adze. Later, built-up sides were added and later still the whole hull was assembled from smaller planks. Examples of all types are still used today.

The main features of the log-canoe were its ease of propulsion, its speed, and its great directional stability, all of which stemmed from its length and narrowness coupled with appreciable depth and grip. However its seaworthiness was not good since it tended to go straight through waves and it was also not easily manoeuvred.

Variations and combinations of these ideas and others produced many better compromises of which the long-boat or gig was typical giving adequate weight carrying capacity with good stability, seaworthiness and handling qualities.

Steering and hull shape

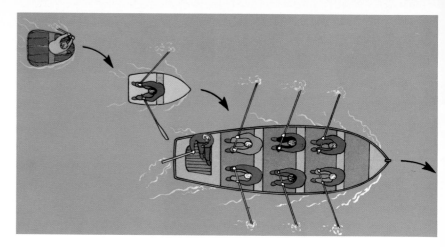

Rafts and coracles were paddled or poled along, but were difficult to steer. Longer and better shaped boats could be controlled by a single paddle or by two or more people paddling together or independently on opposite sides, but a much better and safer development was to use oars. **Steering** and propulsion could be combined in one strong body movement of a single person placed well inboard and centrally. More or less effort on either oar could alter the boat's direction whilst at the same time giving propulsion.

Controlling side-slip

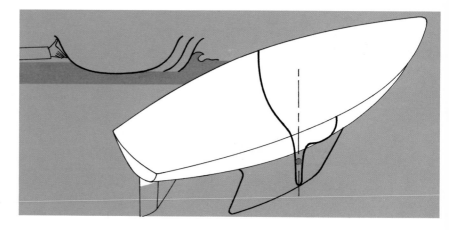

So the normal weight-carrying hull is imprecise in its steering and, in spite of having better grip on the water than the flat raft or the round coracle is still too sloppy and vague in its control.

The types of underwater shapes usually seen today on modern yachts consist of a main hull to which is attached either a fixed fin or a moveable and retractable **centre-board.** There are many variations in detail and sometimes there are two fins side by side, but they all have the twin purpose of improving steering and reducing side-slip.

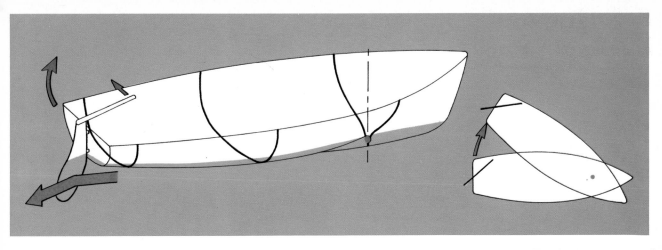

A further refinement which could be applied to all sorts of boats using many different systems of propulsion, was the directional **rudder.** This vertically hinged blade could be angled to the water flow so that the force displaced the **stern** of the boat, to which it was attached, bodily sideways.

At the same time, the hull form of a boat was being developed to become sharper and more flared forward to cut the water and throw spray aside. The sharper entry and deeper sections of the hull gave greater grip on the water but meant that the natural pivoting point of a hull when turning was well forward and the tendency was for the flatter stern to swing unduly wide.

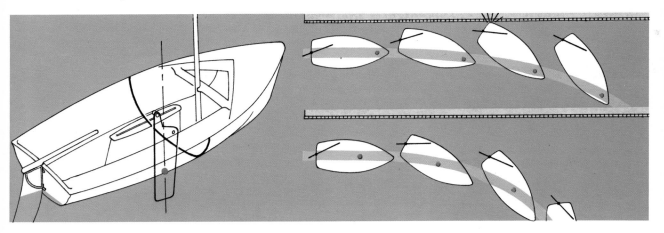

The result of fitting this projection under water is that the hull tends to pivot about its centre of area since it is so large compared with the vertical part of the rest of the underwater hull. The boat turns with less side-slip and is far easier to control.

Also, when travelling in a straight line but under the influence of a steady side-force such as a side wind, the hull with its centreboard or fin has a great resistance to slipping sideways but a negligible extra resistance to moving forward.

Displacement and water-flow

The weight of a boat and its cargo is called its **displacement,** since it is the same as the weight of water that it displaces when floating freely (A). This is identical to the water which will exactly fill its underwater hull shape. So you can make this underwater part of any shape provided its volume is the same. If you put more people or cargo into a boat it sinks deeper into the water and hence the underwater volume increases (B). If the hull shape remains the same you eventually reach a point where you have to build up the sides to restore seaworthiness (C).

Imagine a flat and shallow tray which floats lightly on top of the water. If you push it along, the water hardly has to get out of its way at all. The tray is light to push —it needs very little effort power to move it—it can move fast and even skim over the water provided the weight is low. Speed boats, and also light racing sail boats, have some of the features of the light, flat tray and, in certain conditions, can be made to go very fast for their size and power.

Now imagine a hull, heavily loaded with goods. It sinks deep into the water. If the hull was square ended it would be hard to move since it would tend to push a great deal of water before it and would be held back by turbulence and disturbance behind. So a hull which is not light enough to skim over the surface has to be carefully shaped underwater so that it parts the water in the easiest way, swells out smoothly to give enough volume to carry the required weight, and then comes gently together again at the stern so that the parted water can join again with the least possible fuss.

Such a heavy displacement hull can only be moved at a comparatively slow speed and can never lift out of the water and skim like the tray. Nevertheless there are advantages to both types of hull shape but each has completely different design features.

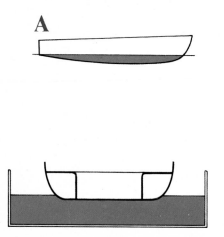

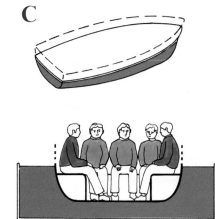

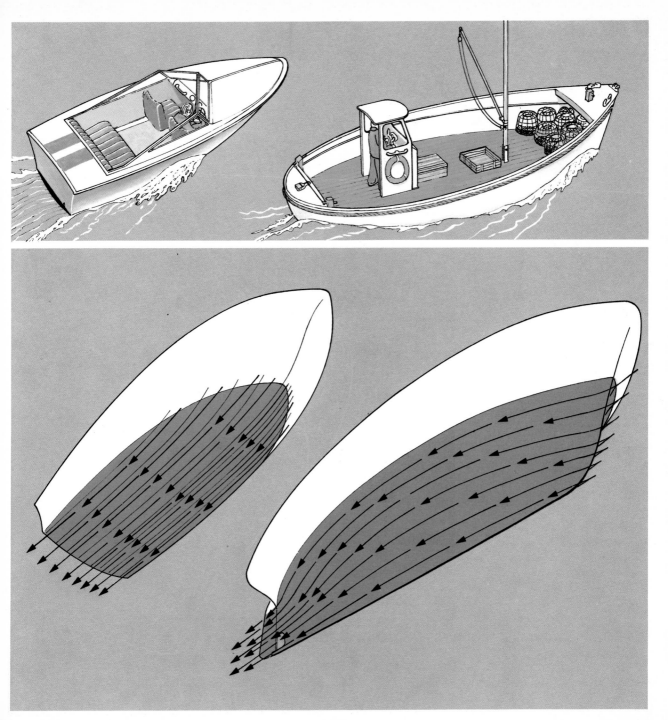

Designing a light hull

The problem in designing a light sailing dinghy is that the overall weight is low enough so that, in strong winds and favourable conditions of sea and with skilled crew work, it is able to react like the tray by lifting up on top of the water and skimming very fast. But for the majority of the time it has to behave like a displacement hull and thus part the water as smoothly and as effortlessly as possible.

In practice, as can be seen on the previous page normal boats need very different hull shapes in the two sets of conditions. But for a light boat which does not need to sink deeply into the water, the designer can take advantage of differences in the **trim** of the hull.

If the boat is first thought of as moving quite level, an underwater hull shape can be drawn to deal with low speed water-flow in an efficient and gentle manner (I).

Now, if the wind increases, and hence the available power becomes greater, the boat can be trimmed by moving the crews' weights so that

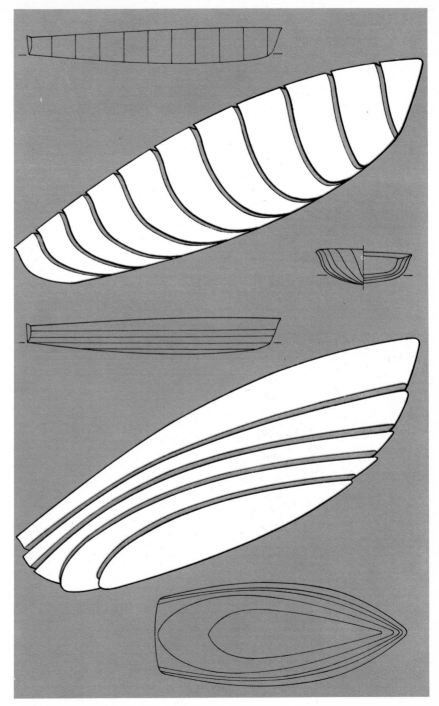

the **bow** lifts and the stern drops slightly (II).

As can be seen this gives a completely different underwater shape, since a great deal of the part forward which is specially shaped for smoothly parting the water is now raised out clear, whilst a broader and flatter area near the stern, which had previously been clear, is now immersed.

In other words the designer has achieved a compromise which can deal effectively with both sets of conditions.

Upper, right:
How the **sections** of a boat are represented on paper. This is known as the 'body plan' or 'body lines.'

Lower, right:
How the **waterlines** of a boat are made up. These drawings show the horizontal waterlines.
From a combination of these drawings a designer can make models or perspective sketches and can work out the effects of alterations in trim.

Boat construction

You will see boats today which are built by a wide variety of methods. All small boats can be built by anyone who has patience, care and a certain amount of knowledge and skill but the main systems fall into three groups.

First, there are what might be called the *amateur* methods (A, B and C). Some of these are easier than others and have been specially designed as home builders kits, one or two of which need exceedingly little skill or expertise. In particular, the stitched-and-glass-taped-ply method used in the *Mirror* dinghy has been perhaps the biggest ever success in the field of amateur boat building. All these methods basically use easily obtainable flat sheets of ply, small size reinforcing pieces, screws and glue, and very little else.

A

B

C

Second, are the *traditional* methods (D, E and F). These need a fair amount of joinery skill, but, with care and knowledge, are within a good amateur's scope. They produce a round bottomed hull, instead of one with angled **chines,** and this is marginally better from the design viewpoint and many people also admire the beautiful shapes obtainable.

Third, are the *moulding* methods (G and H). As the name implies these need a mould to begin with which is virtually a hull itself. The mould has to be made very stiff and is either a male or female replica of the hull to be produced. Owing to the expense of making the initial mould these tend to be factory methods where many exact copies are required. Examples are moulded wood veneer hulls, glass reinforced plastics, injection moulded plastics, and sandwich foam and glass.

However, all of these methods produce perfectly satisfactory boats. The main advantage of the popular moulding methods is ease of maintenance.

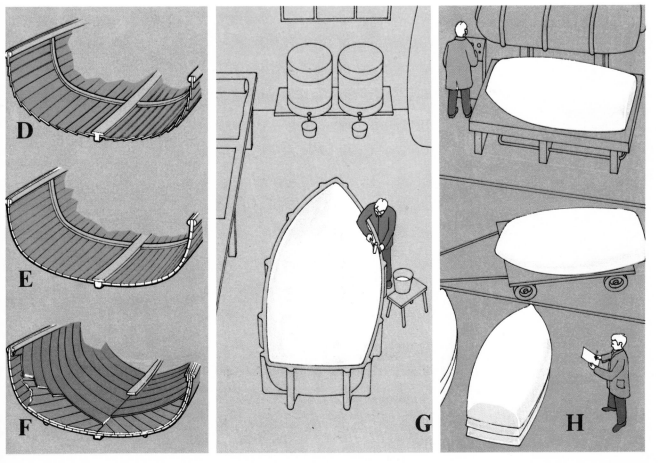

The boat as a wind machine

It was inevitable that the earliest seafarers should have taken steps to harness the free power of the wind to propel their boats. The earliest craft were simply blown along before it and this was practicable provided distances were short and the normal weather gave a sufficient variety of wind directions to use.

But it was gradually found that more elaborate arrangements of masts and rigging, better sail materials and the addition of extra spars and controls, could enable a boat to be propelled by the wind alone at a far greater range of angles to the wind direction than simply straight before it.

At first the main difficulty was holding the baggy sail flat enough. It was found that as one steered further round towards the wind direction the sail had to be angled to keep the wind blowing into it. Eventually one could angle and flatten it no further and the leading edge collapsed as the wind got behind the sail.

The answer to this problem had

been known in principle for some time but the great improvement which could be obtained by hinging the sail at its leading edge could not be made use of since the hull merely slipped sideways as fast as it went forwards.

When better construction methods enabled the side-slip problem to be solved the way was open to a vast improvement in sailing closer to the wind's direction.

The big advantages of the hinged sail were that the great danger of getting out of control when the sails 'blew aback' was gone. The sail simply flapped from its hinged edge and lost power—nothing more. Stemming from this, and coupled with the use of more stable materials, the sail could be held flatter and set at very fine angles to the wind.

Boats actually became able to make progress to some degree towards the wind's direction. This new-found windward ability meant that faster passages were made and less time was wasted in being weather-bound.

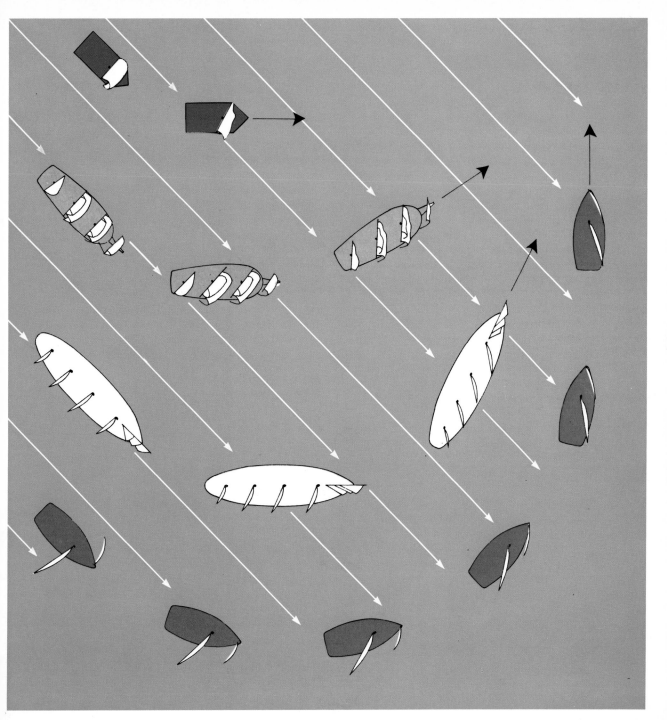

Converting air-flow to sail power

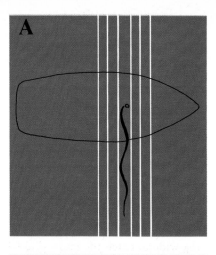

A sail, being made of a more or less soft material, is curved in section when full of wind. There is no need to learn the theory of a sail at this stage but, to sail a boat, one must understand the *effects* of altering the setting of a sail in relation to the wind.

A sail that is flapping produces no power. Therefore if you want to stop your boat you can let the sail flap free (A).

Assume your boat is lying with the wind blowing over one side, since this is the simplest case. Now, pulling the sail to one side of the wind direction causes it to start catching wind (B). First the down-wind edge goes quiet and, if you pull further, more of the sail fills with wind until finally the last little bit at the windward edge 'goes to sleep' (C). It is at this point that the sail develops maximum power as the air-flow over it is *smooth*.

Pulling the sail in is known as **sheeting in** and you will feel the power increase as you sheet in to this point because the boat will try

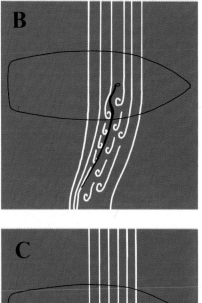

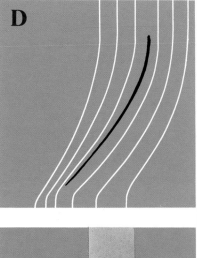

to heel and to move forward.

With *smooth* air-flow you get *push* on the windward side as the sail bends the wind, and you also get *pull* or *suck* from the lee side (D).

If you sheet the sail in closer the air-flow cannot follow smoothly the more abrupt change in direction and becomes turbulent, especially on the lee side (E).

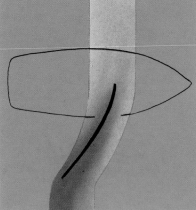

With *turbulent* air-flow the power is reduced because the *pull* fails to operate. You only get *push*.

When the wind is behind you it is hard to avoid this happening but on most other courses you can arrange for the sails to be set so that you get both *push* and *pull*.

Controlling the sails

The modern dinghy uses ropes known as **sheets** to control the angles to which you can set the sails in relation to the boat and to the wind. Hence—'sheet in!' and 'ease sheets!' are the orders often heard. Alternate terms are 'harden sheets' and 'check sheets.'

Normally the two sails are adjusted together at approximately the same angles to maintain the all-important smooth air-flow over both. But when the wind is from behind—or 'from aft'—you can spread your area wide to catch the most wind by setting the sails on opposite sides—or **goosewinging** (F).

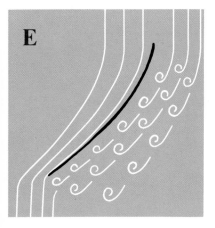

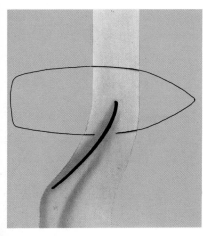

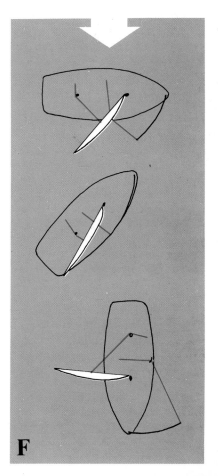

Designing a sail-plan

When designing a sail plan we have to know first the area of sail needed and the number of men in the crew. This fixes the number of sails into which the area has to be broken up and the number of masts required.

But there is also the directional control of the boat and what we call the boat's **balance.** Early sailing ships had very ineffective rudders and they relied to a great extent on the wind's action on the various sails to aid their steering. In fact they could not be controlled without a considerable amount of furling and re-setting of sails. The aim was to balance the wind pressures on the sails to cancel out any tendency for the ship to turn. Or alternately, if turning was what was required, then the necessary sails were set to blow the bow or the stern round.

The modern centreboard dinghy is designed to be very finely balanced when sailing level and, though its steering arrangements are extremely effective, it is very sensitive to pressures acting on the sails which may try to cause it to pivot round its **centre of underwater area.** It simply will not sail properly if there is too much pressure **aft** or too much **forward** of this point.

Large traditional sailing ships carried a very small crew for their size and so the area of canvas had to be split up into many smaller individual sails.

The **square-rigged** *ship used the sails to enable it to turn (A). The rudder of the modern yacht can usually override even the imbalance caused by lowering one sail or the other (B).*

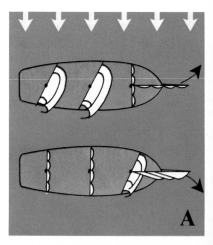

A

The modern offshore racing yacht with a crew of perhaps 9 can be driven hard with the sail area split into only two parts with additional sails for when the wind is aft.

The light two-man racing dinghy also has only two sails plus a spinnaker for use when the wind is astern.

Most singlehanded racing dinghies have only one sail since the one-man crew has quite enough to do in steering and balancing the boat as well as sheeting the mainsail.

*An extra powerful **mainsail** or **jib** compared with its mate can also cause imbalance since it produces more side pressure (C). The remedy is either to adjust the sail's **flow** or to move the whole rig forward or aft.*

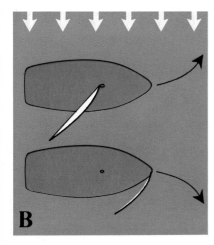

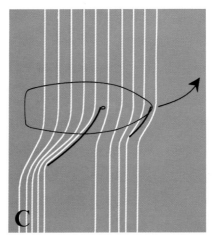

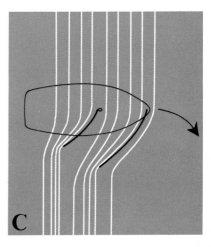

Sail-plans for centreboard boats

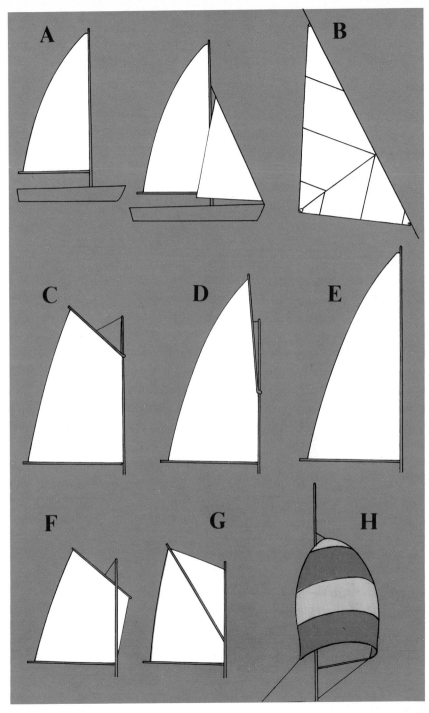

Centreboard boats need to have simple sail-plans and so they only have one mast on which only one or two working sails are set (A). The second sail is clipped (or **hanked**) to the taut wire **forestay** (B). These sails used to be called 'stay-sails' but in small boats are nowadays often referred to simply as **jibs.**

The **gaff mainsail** is used less and less today (C). For small boats the **gunter** sail is more efficient (D), the lower end of the upper part, or 'gaff,' being held to the mast by jaws. The clean and efficient **bermudian** sail (E) was the result of improved mast technology.

For very small boats the **balanced lug** is popular (F), since it is extremely simple and has short **spars** which can all stow within the hull. The **sprit-sail** (G), with its **sprit** holding up the corner, can spread a lot of sail on a short mast.

The **spinnaker** (H) is a very light and baggy sail for catching extra air when sailing before the wind.

Sailmaking

Sails today are made from smooth and stable materials with little stretch. The aim of the designer is to arrive at a shape not unlike the top surface of a bird's wing with a smooth curve from leading edge (the **luff**) (B) to the trailing edge (the **leach**) (D). It should have rather more curve, or **flow,** in the forward part and then flatten off somewhat towards the leach.

The sail is sewn up from **panels** (A) which are individually shaped at their edges. The sewn up sail then also has curves cut on its outer edges. When two of these edges (the **luff** (B) and the **foot** (C)) are fixed to straight **spars** (the **mast** and the **boom**) the sail takes up its designed shape.

The flow in soft sails can be varied to some degree to make the most of varying wind speeds by altering the tension of the **roping** (E) sewn onto the luff and the foot, and further adjustment can be made by allowing a controlled amount of bend to the mast. More tension on the edges flattens the sail and reduces the flow. More mast bend

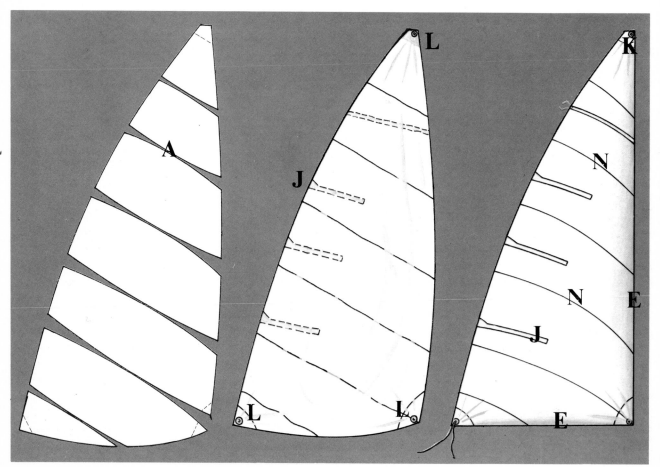

also reduces the power.

Flow control is most highly developed on over-canvassed racing boats which need the maximum power that the crew can handle in all conditions. Boats of this type have a multiplicity of controls and look to the beginner very complicated.

Beginners' dinghies have moderate sail areas for their size, and the rigging and controls are of the simplest. To start with just remember that there should be enough luff and foot tension to remove wrinkles. In harder winds a little more tension on both edges is needed.

Sails should be treated with care. Fold and roll them as shown to keep creases to the minimum. Creases cause disturbance to the smooth air-flow and hence reduce boat speed.

The parts of a sail should be learnt since they will be referred to frequently.

Key:
Sides: luff (B), foot (C), leach (D),
Corners: **head** (F), **tack** (G), **clew** (H),
Other parts: panels (A), roping (E), **batten pockets** (J), **headboard** (K), **cringles** (L), **battens** (M), **seams** (N).

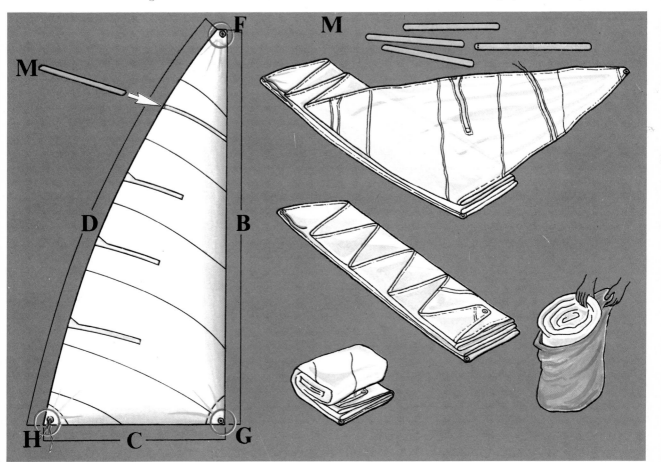

The modern centreboard boat

Our discussion of boats and their development has now arrived at the point where we can consider in detail one particular type—a modern light centreboard sailing dinghy. But even this category is capable of subdivision since, as we have seen, designers can vary the main features of a boat endlessly to obtain the right compromise for their desired purpose.

For example: a *children's* boat will be typically small and light to be easily manageable (8 to 10 feet long), and will have simple fittings and a small sail area of perhaps 45 square feet.

A *yacht's tender* often doubles up for sailing but has to be tubby and tough to carry weight, be a good shape for towing with a swept up bow, but be not too long since it will often stow on deck of a yacht. Its short spars will have to stow within the hull and a lug rig is normal.

A *family* boat will need to be large enough for four people (14 feet and up) and not extreme in any way. The hull shape will be stable and

the sail area moderate. Many types will be suitable for amateur building.

A *racing* boat will have a light hull with a large and efficient sail-plan. The hull shape and all the gear will be very precisely designed and accurately made. There will be a great number of fittings and elaborate controls to adjust minutely the sails and the rig.

The *principles of sailing* are the same for any boat but it is important to remember that a light and powerful boat will show up mistakes instantly and without mercy. But, on the other hand, a slow and stately boat which is comparatively heavy and with a small sail area may be so insensitive that a beginner may not realize when he is doing anything wrong at all.

There are so many types of boats and so many ways of starting that one cannot lay down the law about this. The aim of this pictorial course is to give a thoroughly practical and largely untheoretical background to the principles of sailing and to show in detail how to

manage a typical boat both ashore and afloat. From there on progress is mainly a matter of practice.

Small children learn fast on their own if not frightened. Up to the age of at least ten they usually do best pottering on their own in tiny boats with one sail and also oars and paddle. They will spend hours and days off a shore or jetty just getting the *feel* of the way of a boat on the water—how it floats and moves, and how to move it.

Older children and lively, active adults often do best under the spur of competition, and one way to start is to act as crew for a more experienced beginner in mild club racing. Learning in this way will be fast and perhaps a little brutal at times, but most children will greatly benefit from this and many will then feel confident to get their own boats or to share with another of similar standard.

The more timid or *older person*, or perhaps simply the less competitively minded, may well do best in a heavier boat of a cruising type.

Here we are mainly aiming at the younger beginners who are keen to learn as fast as possible and then maybe move on soon to start racing. Therefore in the pages which now follow we have chosen as our model a typical light dinghy which has all the essentials which can be found on any racing boat but which is not too large or difficult for teen-age crews to manage.

The cockpit
in detail

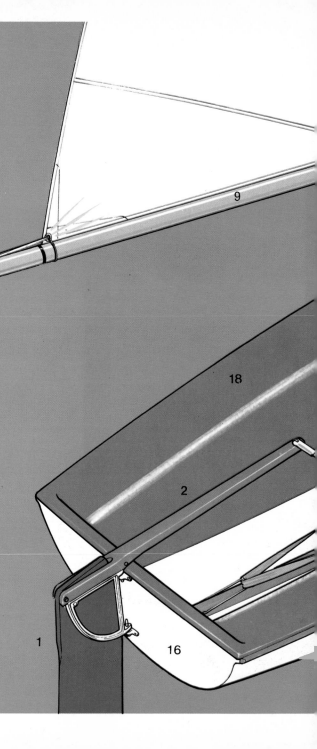

Key to illustration:
1. Rudder
2. Tiller
3. Centreboard
4. Centreboard case
5. Main thwart
6. Mast
7. Mast thwart
8. Mast gate
9. Boom
10. Mainsheet
11. Jib sheets
12. Stem
13. Foredeck
14. Breakwater
15. Gunwale
16. Transom
17. Buoyancy tanks
18. Side decks
19. Bottom
20. Topsides

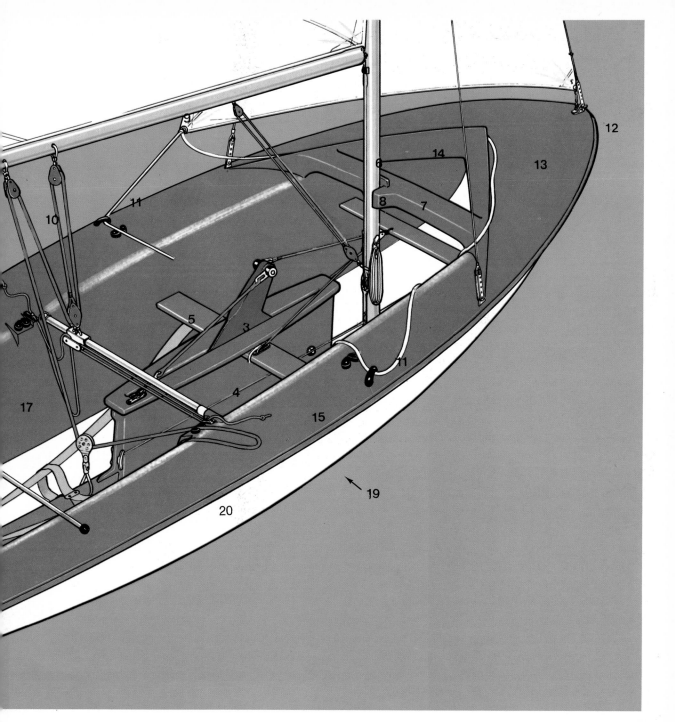

The centreboard

In the introductory part of this book we have seen how vitally important some form of anti-side-slip device is to the sailing boat. Modern small boats use a retractable centreboard or a dagger-board for this purpose and here are shown some typical arrangements.

The simplest is the **dagger-board** (A) which is often found on children's boats and yacht's tenders. The board is raised or lowered by hand and can be pulled right out and laid in the boat's bottom when not needed. A piece of elastic, or **shock-cord,** provides enough friction to hold it in any position when afloat.

The swinging centreboard (B) can be controlled by various arrangements of **uphauls** and **downhauls** (C). In this case the downhaul is a length of shock-cord to keep it down against the drag caused by forward movement of the boat.

In family boats the board often has a simple friction pad (D) made of rubber hose-pipe which can be squeezed to the correct pressure by

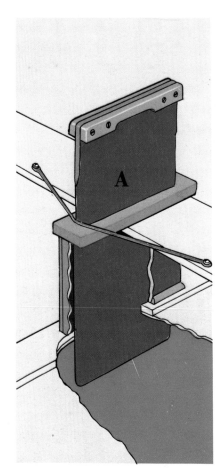

screws with wide washers under their heads. The handle has rubber stops to prevent it being lowered too far (E).

Points to note: ideally the blade should have a special hydro-foil section but in all but top class racing boats a thick plywood blade with a rounded leading edge and a moderately sharpened trailing edge will be quite good enough. However it is extremely important that the plywood is quite flat and not warped, since even a small amount will considerably reduce performance and cause steering problems. Paint the board white to reflect sunlight—a major cause of warping. When making boards out of plywood use either a special type made for the purpose or at least make sure that none of the grain is perpendicular to the leading edge. The bending strain can be high when fully lowered and a board made like this could easily break where it passes the keel.

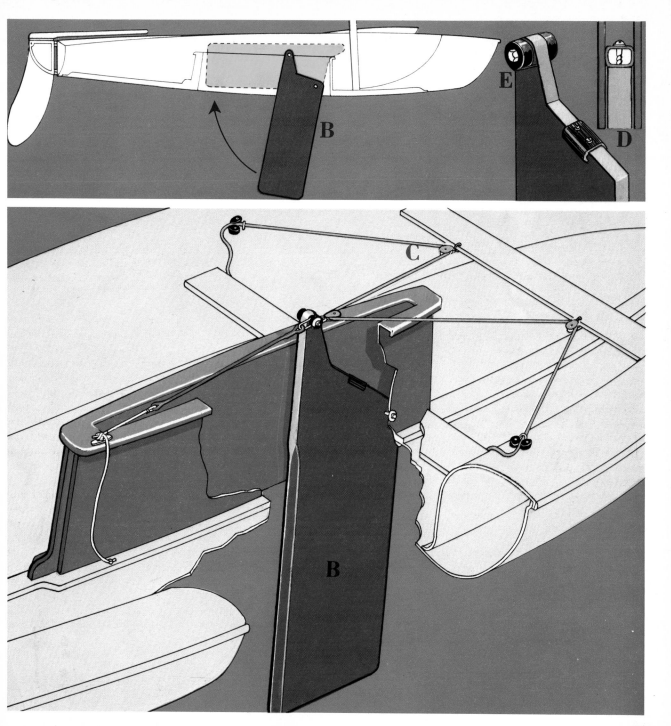

The rudder

The rudder hangings take a very considerable strain and should be strongly made and well fastened. There are several systems of which two well tried methods are shown (A) and (B).

The rules for making the blade are the same as for centreboards and the strongest arrangement is a fixed rudder with a rigidly attached tiller (C). There are big advantages to having a lifting rudder and a lifting or detachable tiller (D), and it is well worth the trouble of having them, but beware of poorly engineered or otherwise inadequate systems.

If the rudder blade is going to lift at all it is sensible to have one which lifts clear of the keel line (E) so that the boat can be fully beached with the rudder in place.

The systems for raising and lowering the blades are often inadequate and, either cannot hold the blade firmly down against the drag of the water flow (a bad and dangerous fault in strong winds), or can develop a degree of slop which is disconcerting to the helmsman.

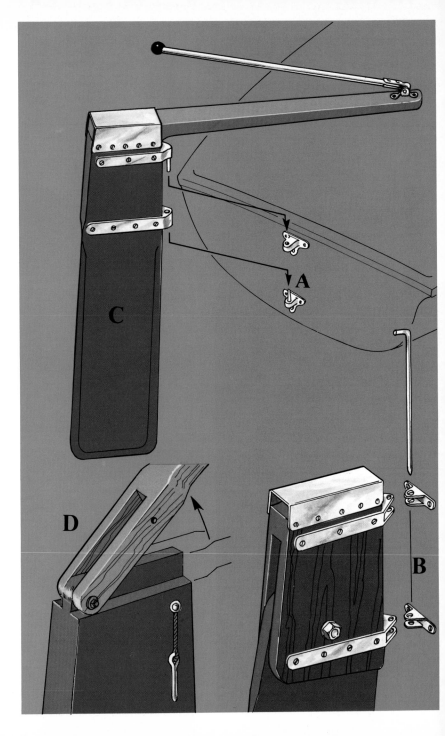

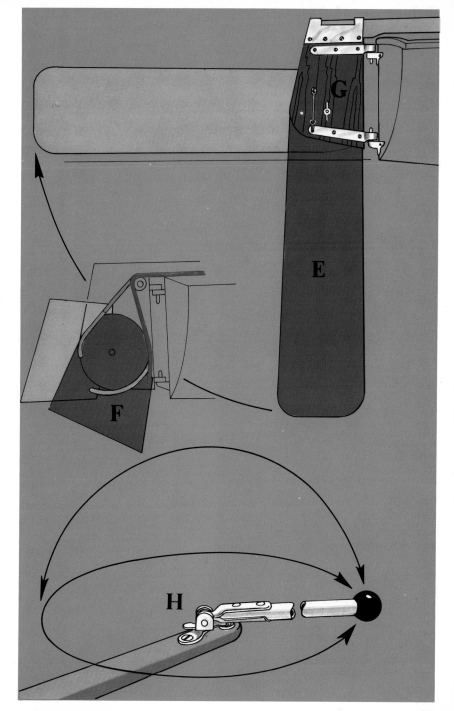

The usual rope and shock-cord system is only suitable for very small boats (F). There are now available very good aluminium rudder heads and tillers with special locking devices to hold the blade firmly down until needed but otherwise far the best solution is a pin on a lanyard which is passed through the blade and rudder head to hold it down (G). A large butterfly nut on the pivot bolt clamps it in the raised position.

A simple but very strong lifting tiller can be made by straddling the rudder blade and hinging it at the aft end (D). The normal sheet-metal hood usually develops slop (C).

Tiller extensions should be fixed with a strong universal joint arranged so that the extension cannot drop below the horizontal (H). They should have a round ball or disc that can be gripped in the palm of the hand with the shaft between the two fingers.

Mainsail sheeting arrangements

A helmsman uses the mainsail control in rather the same way as one uses the throttle on a car to control the power. He needs to be able continually to adjust the sail's angle to the wind in sympathy with the never-ending fluctuations in its strength and direction. It is important that the sheeting system which is selected can match the use to which the boat is put. Simple boats with small sail areas can use simple and more direct arangements, whereas powerful racing boats with large sail areas need more sophisticated systems of ropes, blocks and controls.

Many boats, including most small dinghies and family centreboarders, do not use the central sheeting system (A) since it restricts cockpit space so much. Instead, any one of a number of alternative arrangements can be devised, each having its own special features for particular purposes (B and C). It is worth fitting a system where the final lead comes from forward of the helmsman if possible (D), because then all manoeuvring and changing sides can be done facing forward, i.e. the way you are going. Also it enables another crew member to operate the sheet when required.

Racing boats often have a **traveller** on a track across the centre of the cockpit which can be adjusted for position (E). An alternative arrangement is to have the centresheeting fixed to a central hoop. The number of **blocks** and the way the sheet is led to the helmsman's hand are arranged to give a quick enough response without being too tiring to operate. **Cleats** on the side decks (F) or a swivel cleat on the floor (G) can be used to hold the sheet in any position but they must be arranged to be instantly releasable in the event of a heavy puff or other emergency.

Sometimes the mainsail has to be reduced in area, or **reefed**, and this is done in a dinghy usually by rolling the sail round the boom (H). With a central sheeting system one has to use a **claw-ring** (J) since the normal fixed boom blocks would otherwise be covered by the sail and reefing would be impossible. Most racing dinghies, however, do not ever reef so the use of a claw-ring is limited.

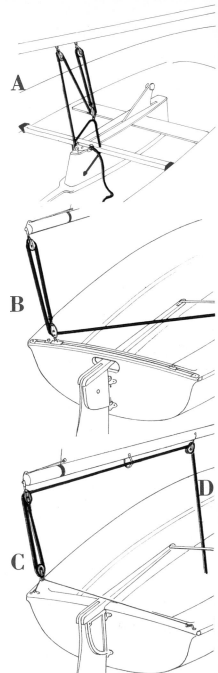

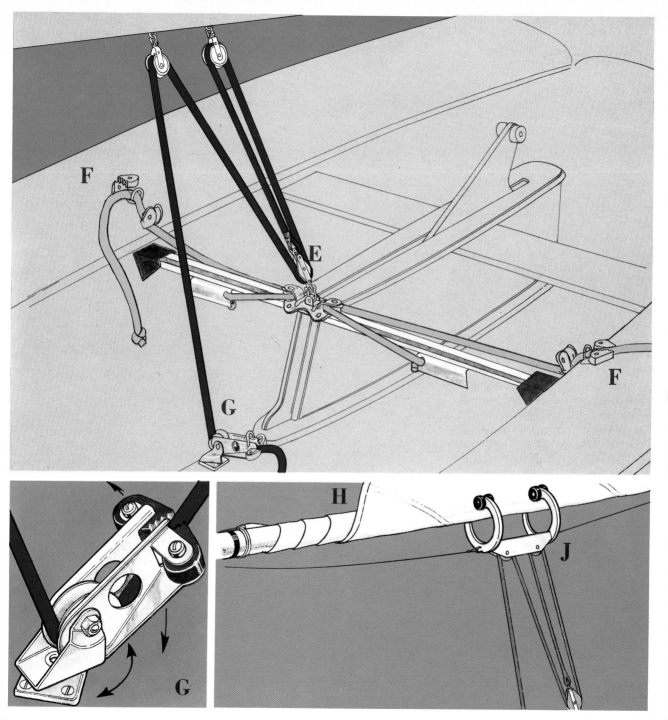

More on mainsheets

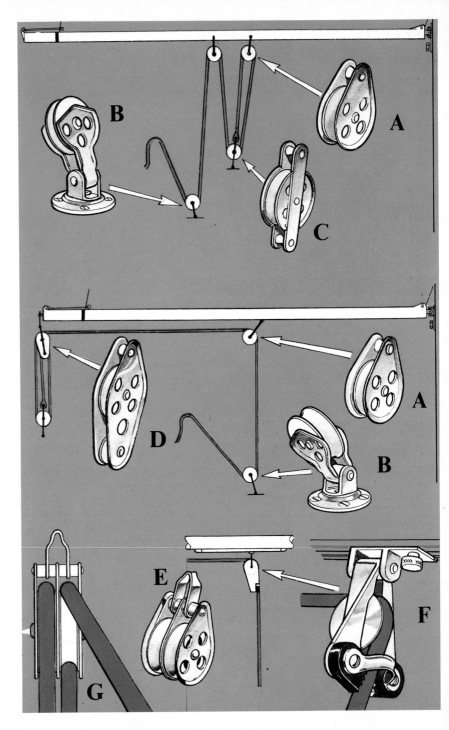

Blocks are used to increase the power of the system. But more power also means more rope to pull in and also more friction. Low friction ball or roller bearing blocks can be used where their expense is justified.

Some points to note: lead the rope correctly so that there is no chafe. Only use **swivel blocks** for the final lead block on the floor. Only use **double blocks** where *all* parts of the rope lead off in the *same* direction—otherwise the block will twist and the rope chafe (G). Instead use a **fiddle block**.

Key:
(A) Single block, (B) Swivel block, (C) Single and becket block, (D) Fiddle block, (E) Double block, (F) Under-boom block with cleat.

The kicking strap or vang

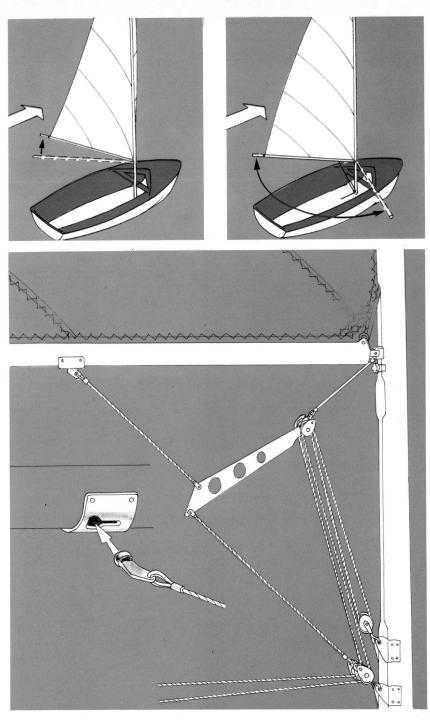

The **kicking strap** is a small but powerful tackle or lever which is used to hold the boom down and take twist out of the mainsail. A boat is far easier and safer to handle, and the sail power is more controllable, if it is free from excessive twist, and so a kicking strap should always be fitted. In fact, nearly all mainsails are designed only to set correctly when an effective kicking strap is in use (vang in US).

Points to note: the forces on a kicking strap and its fittings are very large and so everything should be extra strong. The anchorage point should be on the heel of the mast as low as is feasible. The control line should preferably be double ended with one end leading to each side of the boat to a cleat within reach of the helmsman or crew. If a lever is used it can be prevented from flopping around and kept out of the way of the crew by a length of shockcord tied to it and led to the gooseneck.

Jib sheeting arrangements

The jib is controlled by two single ropes leading from the clew of the sail direct to **fairleads** on each side deck and then to the crew's hands. The maximum area that one man can manage easily without aid is around 35 to 45 square feet. Bigger sails can be controlled by special techniques or with **snubbing-winches**, or **ratchet blocks**, but nearly every dinghy will benefit from quick acting **cam cleats** to hold the sheet temporarily. They are operated as shown (E).

The jib sheet is usually one sheet, centred at the clew cringle and held there by tying a figure-of-eight knot on either side of the clew (A).

The sheet should be passed through the fairlead (B) and then *always* have a **stopper knot** put in the end. The usual knot is a **figure-of-eight** which does not jam and can therefore be undone easily (C). This stopper knot should *always* be used on every line which is used as **running rigging** or on sheets or control lines. It would be stupid to lose the end at a critical moment.

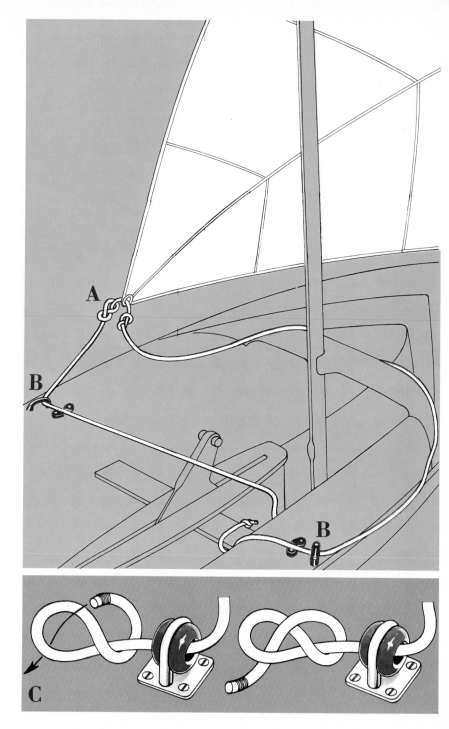

For reasons which will be explained later, it is very important to match the position of the jib fairlead to the particular sail which you are using. If two or more jibs are owned, it is obviously sensible to use some form of adjustable fairlead which can be mounted on a track (D) with a spring-loaded plunger to hold it in various positions. The exact position of the fairlead is critical to good performance when sailing close to the wind's direction.

Points to note: fix the fairlead very securely. Use large diameter rope that is kind to your hands and easy to grip. Never use spirally laid rope with a cam cleat—it will twist out under heavy strain and let go. Site cam cleats so that a pull from a normal direction will automatically release the rope.

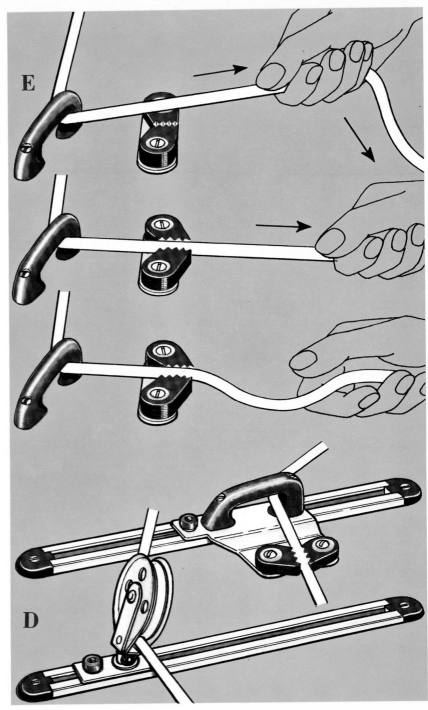

Keeping the cockpit dry

It is vital to keep the boat free of water. A boat is never absolutely upright and if there is free water in the bottom it acts rather like a pendulum, always following the movement of the boat, and then sloshing to the side and trying to pull the boat further over. The more water, the heavier the pendulum, and the more difficult it is to stop the effects of its swing.

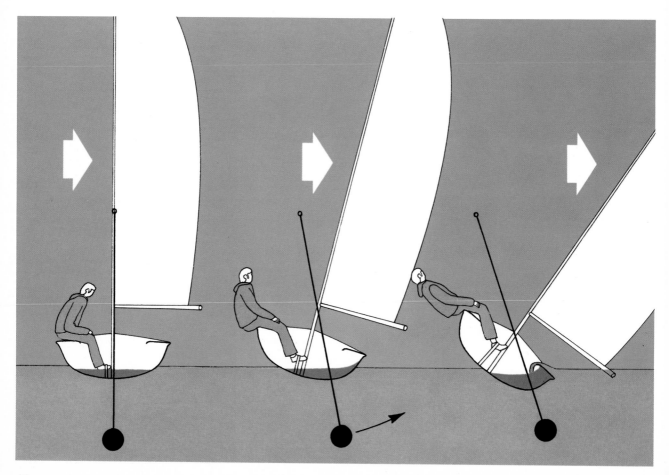

Traditional bailing apparatus are buckets, sponges, and scoops. Use them whenever there is appreciable water in the bilge.

Boats which are not too heavy or too slow, can use one of the semi-automatic **bailers.** This is usually a retractable hollow wedge with a flap-covered hole on the aft side which can project below the boat's bottom. With sufficient boat speed a suction is created and bilge water can open the flap and then fall out into the hollow space.

Racing boats are sometimes seen with flaps in the transom. These are mainly used to free large quantities of water fast. Useful after a capsize to get the worst out.

Points to note: fit bailers at the point where most water collects, modified only so far as to be away from the disturbance of the centreboard (about eight inches minimum) and with protection from the crews' feet (under a thwart).

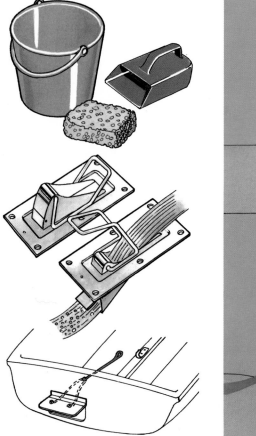

Setting up
the mast

It is always essential for the sailor to know where the wind is coming from and it is a great help to have some form of wind indicator that can be glanced at occasionally. There are many types available from simple flags known as burgees to more sophisticated and sensitive wind vanes. Vanes are usually permanently attached at the masthead (M), but flags are often hoisted on a halyard (Q). Also useful are simple strips of ribbon which can be tied to each shroud at eye level (N).

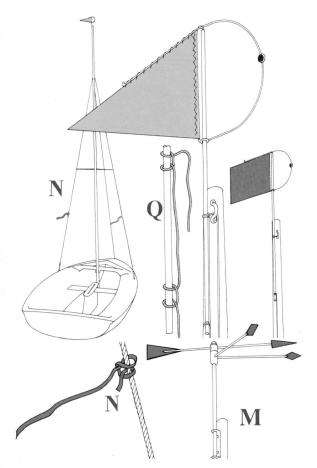

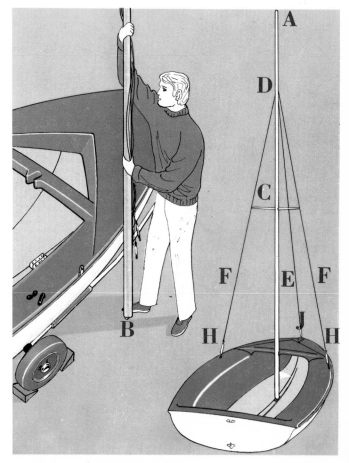

There are two types of mast, **deck-stepped** and **keel-stepped.** The latter can be more easily set up since the **heel** can be placed in the **step** and held whilst the mast is raised vertical. It can then be slipped into the **mast gate** where it is reasonably safe until, first the forestay and then the shrouds, are fixed.

The deck-stepped mast can best be dealt with as shown (L). Chock the boat at an angle to the horizontal. Fasten the forestay and the higher **shroud,** or 'side-stay'. Raise the mast nearly vertical and let the two stays hold it steady. Then raise the heel into the step. Finally fix the other shroud.

A long mast can be raised as shown (K). Stepping a heavy mast may need helpers holding each stay while one or two others lift it into position.

As a last resort the boat can be rolled onto its side, the mast fitted at leisure, and then rolled upright.

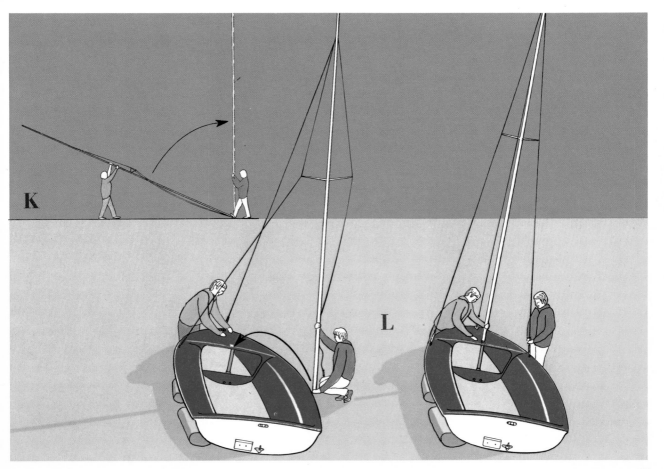

Details of standing rigging

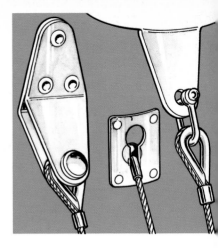

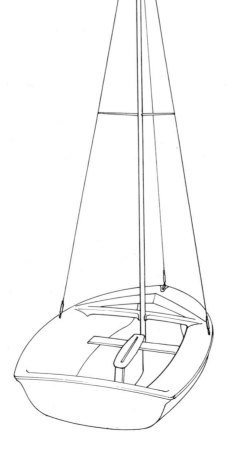

The term **standing rigging** means all those wires and ropes that support the mast and which are fixed at their ends. The main items are the forestay and the two shrouds, or side-stays, but there can also be many other wires and struts depending on the amount of support that the particular rig requires.

The standing rigging needs to be strong, but it is also important for it to be light and to have a low wind resistance. Its strength is that of its weakest link and so, great attention should be paid to the careful fit of end terminals, pins and links. Also, the strength of each part should be matched to that of its neighbours.

Aluminium and stainless steel are the most commonly used materials. Remember that an electrolytic sealer is needed between mast fittings which are made of stainless steel and the aluminium mast itself.

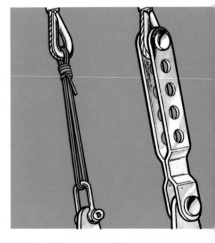

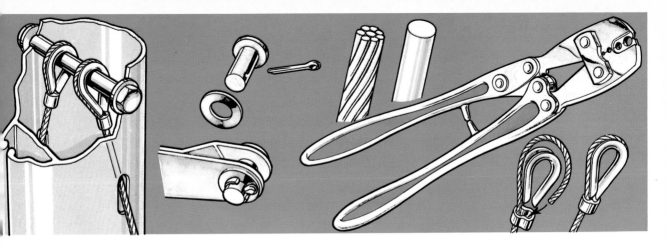

Another neat way of fitting the upper ends of shrouds.

Clevis pins *should fit exactly and without slop or end-play. Fit washers to make up thickness where necessary.* **Split-pins** *should be fitted as shown to avoid snagging. Never re-use a split-pin.*

Standing rigging wire should be of 1 × 19 construction for strength, low stretch and low windage. Solid wire can be used but needs great care to avoid kinks. For clamped terminals use aluminium ferrules with galvanized wire and copper ferrules with stainless steel.

Lower ends need to be adjustable. Synthetic line can be used for small boats. More usual are adjustable **rigging links** *held by pins and spring clips. A better type has increments arranged on a vernier scale so that small adjustments can be made.*

Rigging screws *should have a reliable locking arrangement. Lock nuts are not satisfactory—nor is tape—best is copper wire but remember that one of the threads is left-handed. Put tape or plastic tube over the whole fitting to prevent chafe.*

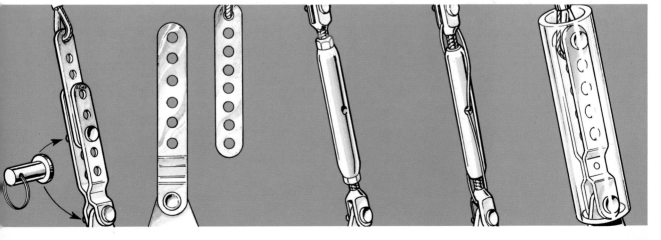

Fitting and hoisting mainsails

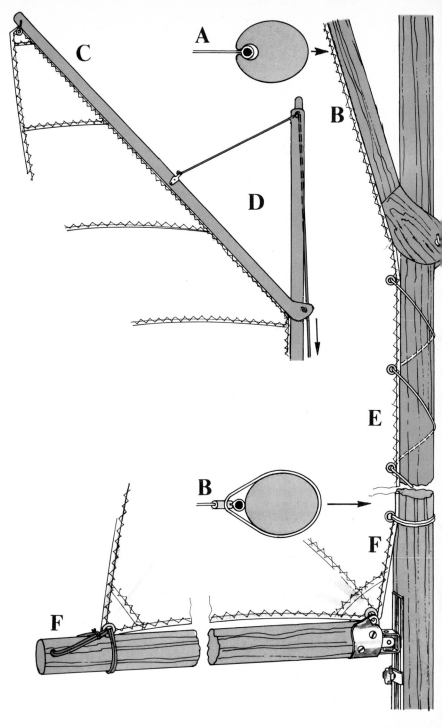

The drawings make this operation largely self explanatory but there are some **points to note:**

With gaff or lug rigs, thread (A) or lace (B) the sail to the gaff (C) first. With gunter-lug rigs (D) the luff should be laced to the mast with a loose spiral lacing (E) which tightens when fully hoisted.

All mainsails, whether set loose-footed or not, should have two or three turns of line around the boom at the clew (F). This is where the greatest strain comes and the sewing of the rope often chafes and becomes too weak to support the load on its own.

Some masts have a metal or plastic track to accept slides sewn to the sail (G). If a pin or stop is put at the lower end the slides cannot fall off when the sail is lowered. Other masts have a groove for the sail roping and if they are hollow the **halyards** can pass down the inside (H).

The universally jointed **gooseneck** (J) has a spike which connects with the boom (K).

For masts and booms with grooves you should have someone to feed in the rope (L).

Put a pin through the boom to hold the tack (O). Adjust the **outhaul** tension (M) and secure with one or two turns round the boom and two **half-hitches** (N).

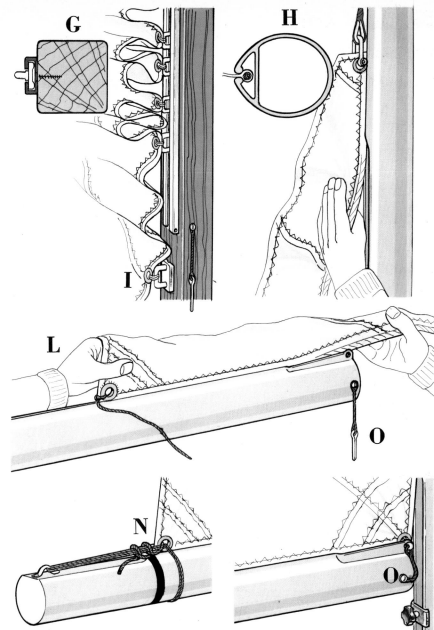

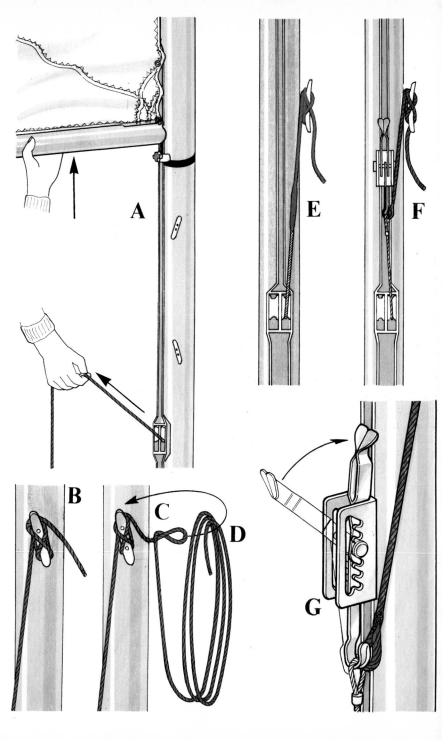

Points to note:

Many dinghies have a sliding goose-neck (A). Lift the boom to help hoist the sail the last bit, and then cleat the **halyard**. Take a full turn around the base of the cleat (B) before making a series of figure-of-eight turns around the horns of the cleat and then coil the halyard. Twist a loop as shown (C) and pass it through the coil and over the cleat (D).

Flexible wire halyards usually have a **rope tail** either **spliced** on (E) or connected to a wire loop, called a **soft-eye** (F).

Instead of making the halyard fast to a cleat, the loop can be hooked into, and tensioned with, a **high-field lever** (G).

When adjusting the tension on the sail luff (H) and foot (J), go by the look of the sail and not the positions of the measurement marks. Above all, never sail without having stretched away wrinkles perpendicular to the spar (K).

Often there is a **cunningham hole** (L) in the sail. A light tackle (M) can pull this hole downwards towards the boom thus putting extra tension on the luff to flatten the sail in hard winds.

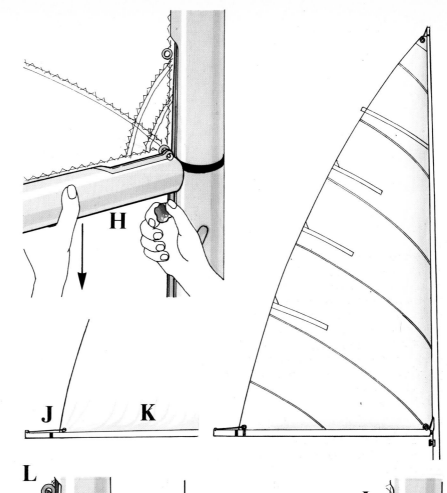

Fitting the jib

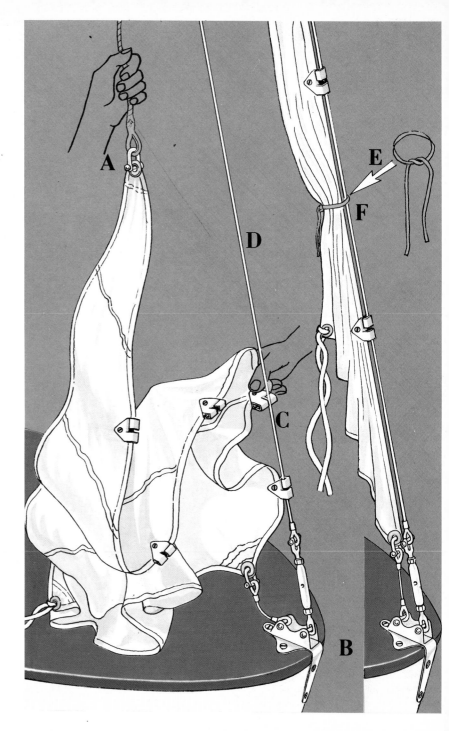

Fitting the jib consists of connecting it to the halyard (A) and stem head (B) and then hanking (C) the luff to the forestay (D). Remember to reeve the sheets and to put a stopper knot in the ends at this stage too.

Some jibs are **set flying,** which means that they have no hanks. It is then extra important to set up the halyards tight enough so that the forestay takes no load at all.

Have some **tyers** handy and wrap them round the sail (E) to stop it blowing overboard before you are ready to hoist.

It is a good idea to hoist the jib then roll it and tie it to the forestay (F). When rolling, keep the leach edge pulled down tight and then roll against the wind.

Sail battens

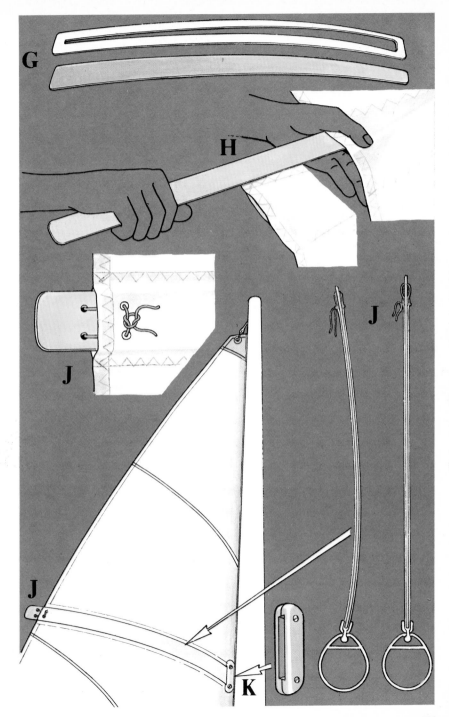

Battens are used to keep the leach of the sail extended and to stop curling or fluttering at the edge (G).

Battens are made of many different types of wood and also plastics and glass fibre. They are tapered so that the forward end is more flexible and this helps the sail to set to the required aero-dynamic shape.

Battens usually are made to slip into elasticated pockets (H). Full length battens have to be tied or held in with Velcro since their tension needs to be adjustable (J).

The upper batten, which shouldn't be tapered, often runs from the leach to the mast where it slots into a special fitting to prevent its end getting jammed into the mast groove (K). The outer end projects several inches so that it can be tied at different tensions. Light tension means that the batten lies flat for hard winds. Tight tying means that when the sail is set, the tension on the leach compresses the batten and forces bend into it for extra sail power in light winds.

Clothes for sailing

The wise sailor will always remember that it is always colder afloat than ashore. It is essential to choose the right clothing for sailing or you will not be comfortable. In dinghy sailing there are two problems —staying dry and staying warm. In stable dinghies which are unlikely to capsize one can wear ordinary clothes to keep warm — such as jeans, a teeshirt and a sweater, underneath a set of oilskins to keep the water at bay. An alternative under-layer is a set of thermal underwear which gives excellent warmth with a minimum of layers. Oilskins for dinghy sailing should be light and not bulky or movement in the boat will be hampered. The best design of suit is the one-piece since it restricts movement least of all and doesn't allow cold air or water in the way that separate trousers and jacket can do. The problem with wearing warm clothes under oilskins is that should you capsize or fall in the water you will immediately get wet and hence cold.

Therefore most keen dinghy sailors wear wet-suits whenever the weather is chilly or if they are likely to capsize. Modern wet-suits are well designed, colourful and do not restrict the wearer in the way that older types

used to. They can be bought in a range of styles to suit the weather conditions in which you are likely to sail and the most versatile arrangement is to have a long-john without sleeves over which you can wear a short jacket when the weather is especially cold.

An alternative to the wet-suit is the recently introduced dry-suit. This garment is made from similar material to oilskins but has seals at neck, wrists and ankles which prevent the ingress of water should you fall in. A heavy duty zip, usually at the back, allows entry and seals the suit. Since water cannot get into a dry-suit it also cannot get out so condensation can be a problem, especially if too much clothing is worn underneath. Thermal underwear is ideal for use with a dry-suit in winter and the amount worn can be adjusted to suit the weather conditions and the amount of exercise you are likely to have to do. Many sailors wear a light overall over a dry- or wet-suit to protect the valuable sailing suit from damage. By choosing the colour of the overall carefully some control of body temperature can be obtained. Thus a white overall in summer will reflect the sun's rays and stop you overheating while a blue one in winter will help retain much wanted heat.

Footwear is also of great importance since not only does it protect your feet from damage but it also provides the grip you will need on slippery surfaces. Ordinary plimsolls can be worn but proper sailing shoes or boots—either short or long—will prove more satisfactory and longer wearing. You may also find that a pair of sailing gloves helps protect your hands and you could also find use for a pair of sunglasses and a good strong sailing bag in which to carry and stow all your gear.

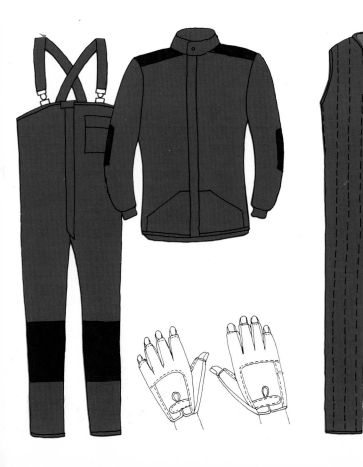

Buoyancy aids and lifejackets

As with all watersports the ultimate risk when sailing is from drowning and all dinghy sailors should wear some form of personal buoyancy whenever they are afloat. There are two main types of personal buoyancy garment: lifejackets and buoyancy aids.

A lifejacket is a garment that will provide full support for a person in the water and will automatically turn the person onto his back with his head held clear of the water. In order to provide support that does not require the person to tread water or to swim, a proper lifejacket has a minimum of 35 lbs (16 kg) of buoyancy.

Many different types of lifejacket are available but a popular type is the inflatable lifejacket (I) which folds flat against the chest when deflated. The problem with this type is that it must be inflated when needed, either by mouth or gas inflation. It is not too easy to inflate a lifejacket by mouth when in the water but gas cylinders need regular checking to ensure that they are still capable of inflating the jacket.

Lifejackets with full built-in foam buoyancy can be used but they are very bulky and do restrict movement in the boat. If partial built-in support is thought necessary jackets can be obtained with about half the buoyancy provided by foam blocks with the rest given by inflatable pockets.

The important thing about all lifejackets is that they position the majority of the buoyancy on the chest so that the wearer will always float on his back even when unconscious. The remaining buoyancy is in the collar to support the head clear of the water

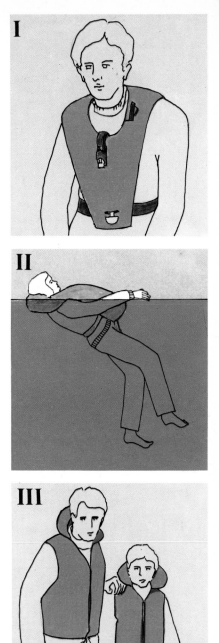

(II). The problem with this disposition of buoyancy is that it gets in the way when worn in the boat (unless the lifejacket is deflated) and can also make it very difficult to climb into a dinghy from the water.

Buoyancy aids (III) come in a variety of shapes and styles and also provide the wearer with differing degrees of support. Unlike a lifejacket, a buoyancy aid is, as its name implies, only an aid to swimming and need not have the full 35 lbs of buoyancy required by a lifejacket. Typical amounts of buoyancy vary between 14–22 lbs. (6.5–10 kg).

Buoyancy aids are usually made as waistcoats with the buoyancy, in the form of blocks of closed-cell foam, spread evenly front and back. There is usually a large collar to help support the head and the jacket is usually fastened by a zip or straps. If a zip is used there should also be at least one strap or tie fastener for safety purposes. There should also be crutch straps to keep the jacket in position.

Although the buoyancy aid gives only partial support in the water and does not turn the wearer onto his back, this can be an advantage to the dinghy sailor who will want to be able to move around his capsized dinghy without difficulty. Because the buoyancy aid has its buoyancy spread throughout the jacket it is less bulky and can look more stylish than the lifejacket.

Which type is chosen is a matter of personal preference — racing sailors will usually chose a buoyancy aid for mobility while the person who cruises in a dinghy is likely to wear a lifejacket for ultimate safety when away from club rescue services. The chosen make should be comfortable to wear and easy to put on. The fastenings should be absolutely secure and reliable and there should be a whistle attached to the jacket so that a person in the water can attract attention.

Buoyancy in the boat

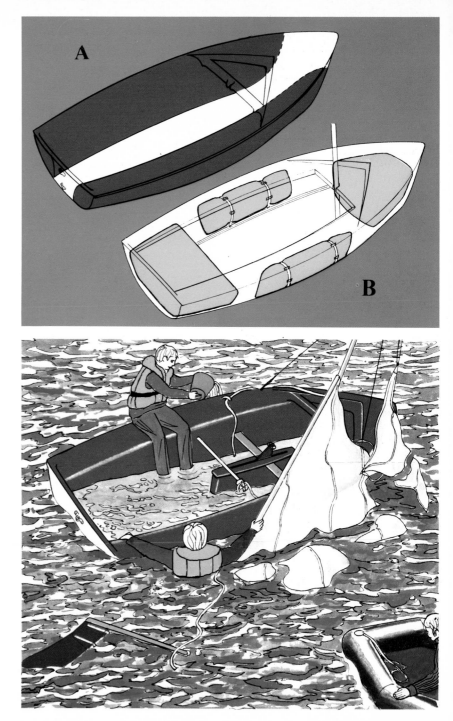

Virtually every small boat now-adays is designed to have built-in surplus buoyancy in the form of **air tanks** (A), slabs of closed-cell foam, or sandwich mouldings filled with foam. In the comparatively rare instances of there being no built-in surplus, then it can be added by using special **air-bags** which are made in many shapes and sizes (B).

This surplus buoyancy enables the boat and its crew to remain afloat even when fully flooded or capsized. But it is essential to give it a certain minimum inspection and maintenance if it is to do its vital job in the, always unexpected, emergency.

There is an ideal quantity of surplus buoyancy for any boat. Too little and a swamped hull will be unstable and may not support the crew. Too much and the boat will float so high that the crew may not be able to climb on board, it will turn upside down too easily, and the boat may blow down wind faster than the crew can swim after it.

The disposition of the tanks is

also important. Large bow and stern tanks plus smallish side tanks (B) is the best arrangement for safety and ease of righting. Other arrangements have certain advantages in racing boats but the correct righting drill must be learnt.

Before you go afloat you should be satisfied that the boat really will float. Why not give it a trial in the harbour?

We shall be discussing capsizes and righting techniques in detail in Part Three. At this stage there is only one 'Golden Rule':

ALWAYS STAY WITH YOUR BOAT

You are safest with the boat. Never try to swim ashore—so many have tried, and so few have made it. With the correct technique—explained later—nine times out of ten a capsize is only a temporary and damp delay to your sail, and you will be able to get going again within half a minute or so. But if, for some reason, you are unable to rescue yourself, sit tight and await help.

Points to note:
Clip or pin the rudder in place. If the boat goes upside down it will otherwise fall off and you may lose it. Secure all loose gear with short lashings.
If you lower the sails always secure them by wrapping with a line. Motorboats will not approach until you have recovered all trailing lines and sails.
If sitting on the upturned hull get hold of the end of one of the sheets to hang on to.

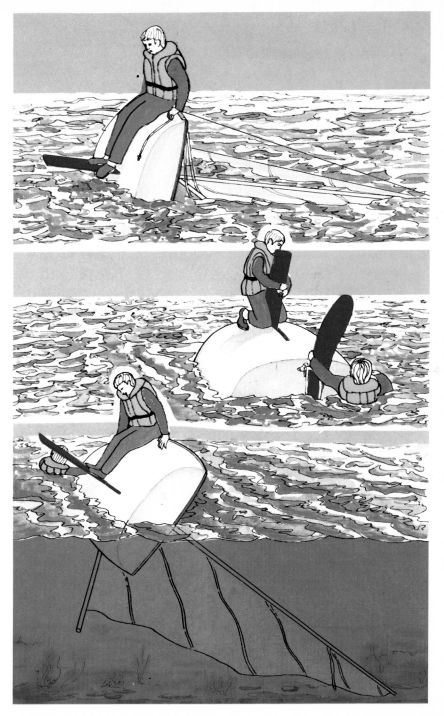

Handling boats on shore

Boats are meant to float and everything about them is designed with this in mind. They can be awkward to manage ashore unless the right equipment and techniques are used.

Boats are light and so why not carry them on the car roof? Three or four helpers are normally needed but a boat can be pushed up on top with two people if a roller is fitted on the roof rack.

Roof racks should be of the special type which fit into the roof gutters and must be well secured. Take the boat's painter down to the front bumper and another line to the rear, for extra security.

A roller on the **trailer** also simplifies handling on and off. Trailer wheels are rarely sealed adequately enough for immersion so a light **trolley** is very useful in addition.

The bearing point on the **trolley** axle should be as low as possible to make it easy to slip under the hull. Chocks should be long and wide to spread the load over the bilge and not the flat part of the bottom.

Roller bearings run best but plain ones are adequate if frequently greased. Inflatable, or at least sponge, tyres are essential. Special wide sand wheels should be of large diameter.

Remember to protect the boat's bottom when resting the hull on the ground or when launching off a jetty. When moving a boat on a trolley make sure that the bow of the boat is tied to the trolley with the painter so that the boat cannot slip back off the trolley.

Launching and recovery

Just as handling a boat on shore can be made as easy as possible by using the right equipment, so can launching the boat into the water be made relatively painless by using the right techniques. In emergency and with careful preparation, all these methods can be used single handed, but they are so much easier with more helpers.

I. When pushing or pulling a boat on a trolley over difficult ground always get hold of the trolley and not the boat, which can slide about unless well lashed down. Go stern first into the water with the **painter** (the line fastened to the bow) held in the hand. When the boat is about to float give it a sharp push while still holding the painter and then quickly pull the trolley out of the way. Finally pull in the boat using the painter.

When recovering, float the boat onto the trolley and tie the bow down to the handle before pulling the trolley ashore.

II. The air rollers make it easy to get the boat across soft sand and shingle. Launch bow first with the rudder fixed and the blade raised. When the water is reached, one member of the crew must hold the boat head to wind until the sails are set, then he pushes off and climbs in. Sometimes, paddling offshore is easiest, the sails being hoisted when clear.

III. Steady the boat with **bow** and **stern lines.** Arrange the slings so that the boat is slightly bow heavy to keep the mast clear of the crane jib.

Before recovering, bail out the water which could otherwise be heavy enough to damage the bottom. Also remove the rudder and raise the centreboard.

Remember to close transom drain holes and bailers when launching.

Paddling

One of the trickiest parts of handling small light boats is getting away from or returning to the shore. Often the only way is to **paddle** off and this is certainly to be recommended for a beginner since he can get clear of obstructions and organize himself before hoisting sails.

A light dinghy with centreboard raised has very little grip on the water. It behaves like the coracle and, if paddled by one person in the normal fashion, will simply spin (A). Lowering the centreboard only provides a pivot around which the hull can still spin.

If you are alone in the boat there are two main ways of getting the boat to go straight.

First, you can fit the rudder and tiller, sit on one side deck and start paddling (B). The tiller will immediately swing your way as the boat tries to spin but you stop it with your outstretched knee and, keeping the tiller straight, continue paddling.

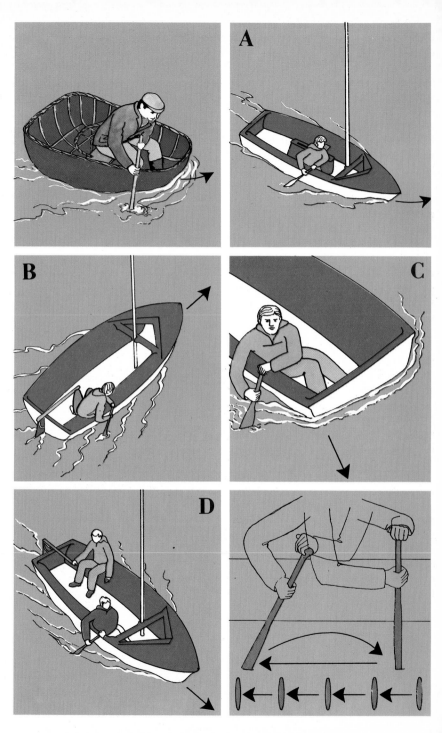

The second method is simpler since you can jump in and set off without having to fit the rudder, but it can only be used in reasonably smooth water. In this, you paddle stern first sitting aft on the side deck (C). The secret is to. *pull* the boat along using the paddle. The boat will travel slightly diagonally with the corner of the transom leading.

The most satisfactory and powerful method however is to have one person steering and the other sitting further forward and paddling (D). In this way the paddler can concentrate all his strength on propulsion whilst the other can deal with all problems of steering and also balance the boat.

There is a fourth method which is a type of **sculling** action in reverse (E). Kneel or stand facing aft. Grasp the paddle firmly half way down with one hand. This hand provides the power. The other hand grips the hand-hold at the top and is the controlling lever (F).

The power hand simply sweeps the paddle from side to side parallel to the transom (G). The control hand does two jobs—it keeps the paddle vertical and it controls the angle of the blade. At exactly the end of each stroke a sharp movement of elbow and wrist turns the blade for the next stroke.

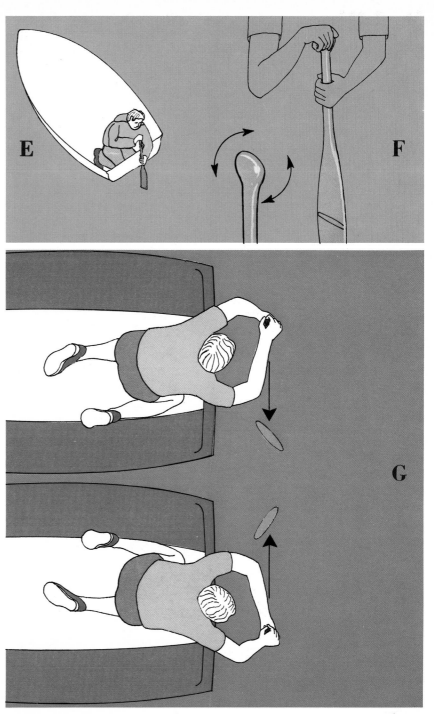

Hoisting sails afloat

We can hoist sails ashore and put the boat afloat fully rigged, but this is only suitable in calm conditions. More usually we set sail once we are afloat and this can be done in two main ways.

I. The boat is on open water. The rudder is fixed, and the centreboard is down. The helmsman holds the tiller and points the boat about 40° to the wind direction.

The crew now has to hoist the sail and rig the kicking strap whilst the helmsman concentrates on keeping the boat balanced and steady. Finally the jib can be set and the boat is ready for sailing.

II. The other method is to paddle to a jetty or other fixed object and tie up temporarily using the painter. Find a position where the boat can lie head to wind and then pass the painter round a **bollard,** or **ring bolt** and back outside a shroud to be tied to the thwart. The boat will now lie at a slight angle to the wind making it easier to hoist sails with the crew sitting centrally, and the boat can be let go from inside.

Don't lower the centreboard at this stage or the boat will try to sail about before you are ready.

The crew can hank on the jib, if it is not already hoisted and rolled, or can steady the boat from the jetty by holding the forestay.

The helmsman hoists the mainsail, adjusts it and sets up the kicking strap, and then fits the rudder and makes sure that everything is correctly rigged.

The jib can now be hoisted or it can be left until after the boat has got underway. Finally the mainsheet is freed right off and the centreboard is lowered. The crew can then turn the boat and, with the sail still flapping, he steps aboard.

The actual sailing of the boat will be explained in Part Two.

I

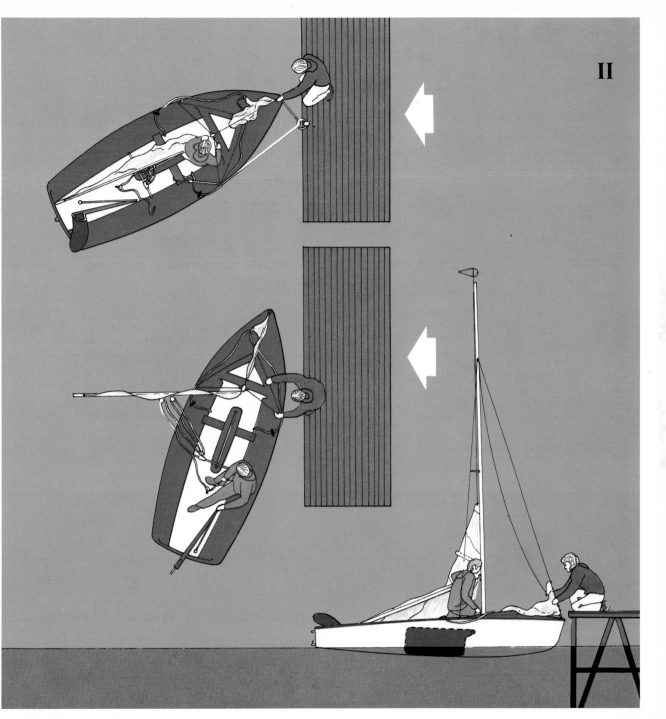

Parking ashore and mooring afloat

Very few light dinghies are stable enough to remain afloat safely on open moorings. They are better brought ashore, or, if left afloat, they can be unrigged and the mast taken down.

However, if you are going to moor alongside, remember that you need **fenders** (A), **bow and stern lines** (B), and also **springs** (C), which stop the boat moving fore and aft.

When mooring between a pier and buoys or posts you should use twin bow and stern lines where possible to control the boat's position.

When leaving a boat on a trolley or trailer, prop up the bow and chock the wheels (D).

Lash the boat onto the trolley (E).

Open transom holes to drain out rainwater (F).

Tie a cover over the boom to prevent pilfering and damage from sun and rain (G).

Some useful hitches are shown for use in securing to various objects (lower, right).

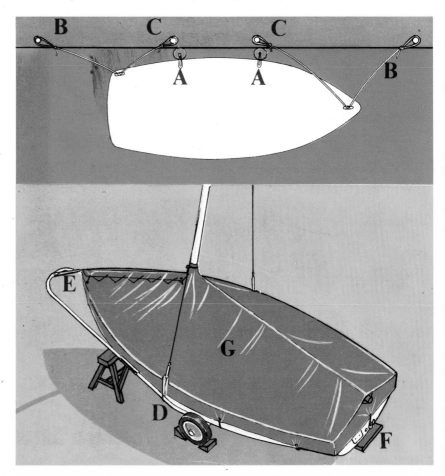

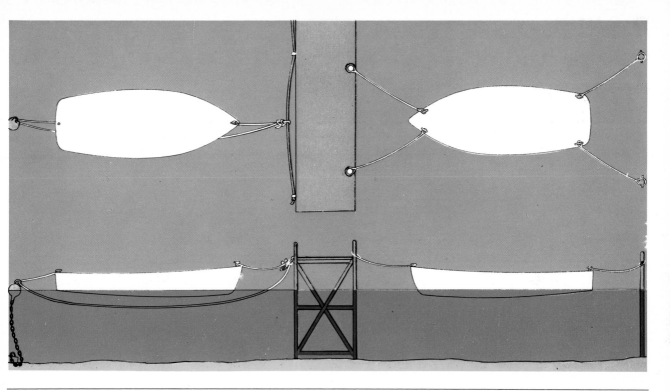

Turn up on a cleat with cross-over turns and a **locking half-hitch** (H).

To secure to a rope use a **rolling-hitch** (J).

The loop to throw over a mooring post is called a **bowline** (pronounced bo-lin) (K).

On a ringbolt use a **round turn and two half-hitches** (L).

Finally, a useful hitch for many purposes is the **clove hitch,** essentially just two half-hitches on top of each other (M).

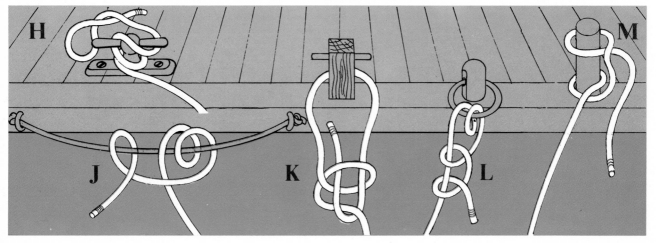

Cruising and safety equipment

Though we are mainly here considering the type of light and lively dinghy which is used for club racing, we should not forget that day cruising or coastal passage making is also within the capabilities of some types of centreboard boats.

We must frankly face the fact that many types of modern dinghy are not suitable for cruising other than very local trips in company. Our model is one of these. Not only is it light but it is over-canvassed for cruising and cannot safely carry the extra equipment which is necessary.

There are excellent centreboard boats of around 16 feet in length which are suitable, with careful preparation, for very long passages. Open sea voyages are possible and one such boat even sailed by stages from England to Australia in 1970. But even for more modest trips most of the illustrated equipment would be virtually essential.

Obviously our small dinghy cannot hope to carry all this. What then, should be essential extra gear

for our boat if we contemplate short trips on our own?

Apart from adequate clothing and personal buoyancy it would certainly be sensible to carry a small waterproof bag with a knife, wire cutting pliers, screwdriver, tape, signal flares and compass. Additionally one or two paddles, bailer and sponge and some emergency rations.

Anchors

Carrying an anchor and line in a small dinghy is a problem as there is really nowhere to stow it where it does not get in the way and, unless thoroughly lashed down, it can slide about and punch holes in the buoyancy tanks. Also, if you capsize, it can drop out and either anchor you when you are not wanting to, or make an additional difficulty for self rescue. However, a useful type of folding anchor is illustrated.

Any size of boat could benefit by anchoring in a calm when the current is carrying one out to sea or towards rocks or shoals. But it is quite another thing to anchor a capsized boat. The drag of a swamped or half sunk boat is enormous and one must never underestimate the strains involved.

The boat can be pulled under water until the current eases, and this could make your situation worse than it already was.

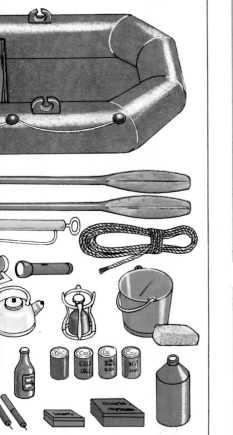

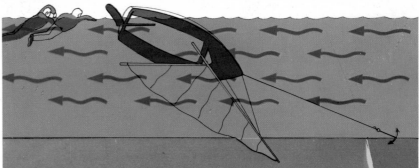

Some nautical terms

Port and Starboard

It is the almost universal custom afloat to use the word 'port' instead of 'left' and 'starboard' for 'right.' These terms are only used when related to a boat and are correct when looking from the stern towards the bow.

You will find later that two important colours are allocated to these terms and are used in right of way rules concerning lights—the left side or *port* is given *red* as its colour. You can perhaps remember that port wine is red and red is *danger. Starboard* is *green* and green is *go ahead.*

Learn these terms and colours and we will explain their other uses in later chapters.

Bearings

To say that some object bears **ahead** or **astern** means that it is in front or behind, and will be familiar to everyone.

We talk about the **starboard bow** meaning, to the right hand side of the bow, and so an object **on the starboard bow** would be somewhere ahead and to the right.

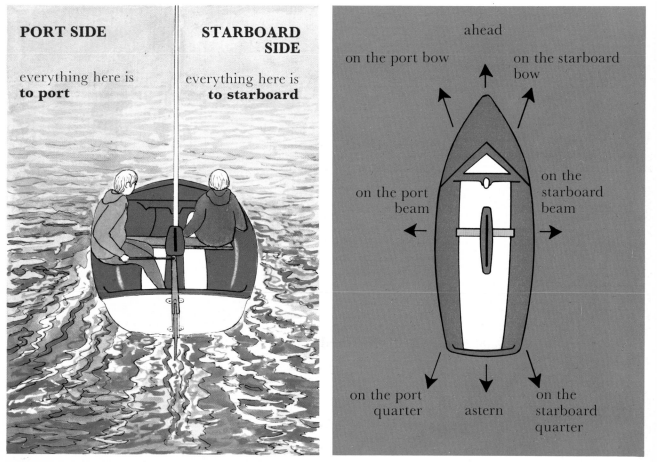

PORT SIDE

everything here is **to port**

STARBOARD SIDE

everything here is **to starboard**

ahead

on the port bow

on the starboard bow

on the port beam

on the starboard beam

on the port quarter

astern

on the starboard quarter

The width of a boat is called the **beam,** so in the direction of the beam, or **a-beam** means towards that side. 'A-beam to port' would mean straight over the left side. Or, 'on the port beam.'

The **quarters** of a ship are the corners near the stern. So 'on the starboard quarter' means, away in a direction astern and to starboard.

The wind

From you towards the wind direction is **to windward** or **up wind.**

From you towards where the wind is going is **down wind** or **to leeward** (pronounced loo-ard).

If you are on the water then any object to windward of you can be said to be a **windward** or **weather** object. Thus: weather shore, windward boat.

Objects to leeward are for example: leeward boat, **lee shore.**

Sailing terms

The only other terms you need to know at this stage are some directions relating mainly to the special case of a sailing boat.

Unless the wind is exactly dead ahead or dead astern, then one side will have wind blowing on to it to some degree. This is the 'windward,' or windy side, also called the 'weather' side. The other is the leeward, or lee, side.

If we push the tiller towards the lee side, or **a-lee,** this means that the boat will turn to windward or, in this drawing, to port.

Pulling the tiller to windward, or to 'weather,' will cause the bow to go to leeward or, in this case, to starboard.

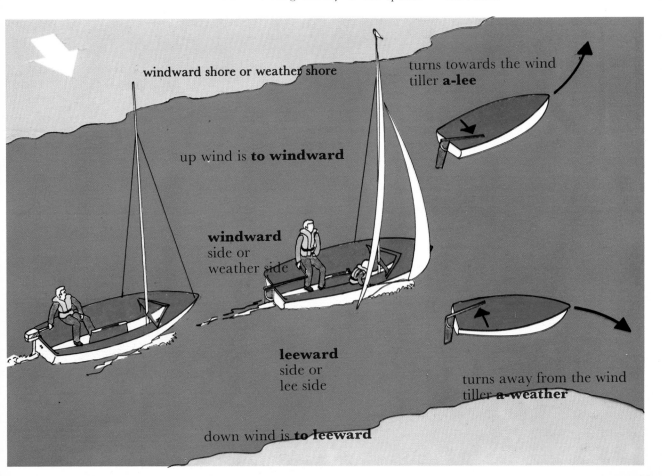

windward shore or weather shore

turns towards the wind
tiller **a-lee**

up wind is **to windward**

windward
side or
weather side

leeward
side or
lee side

turns away from the wind
tiller **a-weather**

down wind is **to leeward**

Two The First Essential Skills

Gathering speed and slowing down

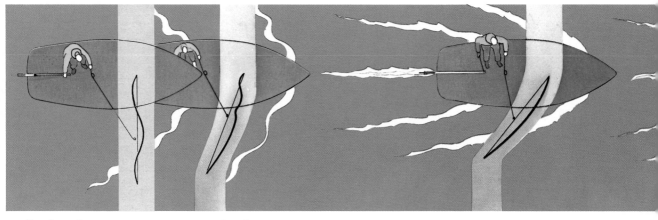

Our boat is on the water—How do we start sailing?

In Part One we saw how the boat was launched and, either paddled into open water where the sails were hoisted, or rigged when tied to a fixed object, and the boat was then turned with flapping sails till the wind came over one side or the other. So this is the position where we are now. The wind comes over the *port side*.

We also saw introduced in Part One the idea that the curved sail

bends the wind flow out of its normal path. Try to imagine the air-flow lines trying to get back into position again and thus they *push* the sail out of their way. The faster the wind is moving, and the bigger the sail, the greater is the *push*.

It follows that, if you start with the sail flapping free and then gradually sheet-in you will get a gradually increasing *push* until you reach a maximum when the sail is full of wind.

But there is also the other major

effect of air-flow on curved sails which acts on the lee side. We said that, if we can establish a *smooth* air-flow over the lee side at the same time as the sail is blown full of wind from the windward side, then the power from the wind on that particular sail is greatly increased.

The problem for the beginner is to know exactly when the lee side air-flow is *smooth* and when it breaks down and becomes turbulent.

There is a guide which is true for all types of sail. If you start

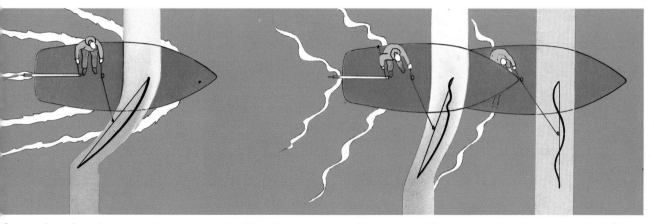

from the flapping position and gradually sheet-in then the down-wind edge of the sail fills first, extending steadily towards the luff until finally this leading edge 'goes to sleep.' It is at this point that *smooth* air-flow is finally established. And it is at this moment that you get maximum power because the *smooth* lee-side air-flow then *pulls* in addition to the windward side's *push*.

We went further and said that, if we sheet in more, we reach a point where the lee-side air-flow can no longer follow the abrupt change in

its direction and becomes unstuck and turbulent. The sail is said to be 'stalled.' The *pull* effect fails to operate.

This is why sailors need to be able to 'see the wind'. This means that you must try to visualize the invisible air-flow all the time. You should constantly think of the direction of the wind and imagine how it is flowing over and behind the sails and then passing away to leeward.

If you can do this, sailing a boat

will be easy for you, so look at this drawing and see if you can *feel* that, as you sheet in, the boat accelerates, and as you ease the sails out again, the boat slows down.

So, the first important skill is this, but you need to know a little more before you can practise this on your own in your own boat, and so read on.

The crew balances the side forces

We are thinking now of a boat positioned so that the wind is coming more or less directly over one side. Remember from Part One that in this drawing the wind is on the *port beam*. The sail is to *starboard*.

The total force developed by the sail is always approximately at right angles to the chord of its curved section. You can assume that the boom nearly represents this chord. (*Top row:* I *and* II.)

With the sail set like this you can see that this **total force** acts in some degree to one side of the boat's centre line. It can be split into two parts—**forward force** and **side force** (III).

The side force alone, causes the boat to **heel** and this is resisted partly by the natural **stability** of the hull but, in a light dinghy, mainly by moving the crew's weight (IV).

Therefore, as you sheet in the sail to move off, you have to move your body outboard to counteract the heeling effect (V, VI and VII).

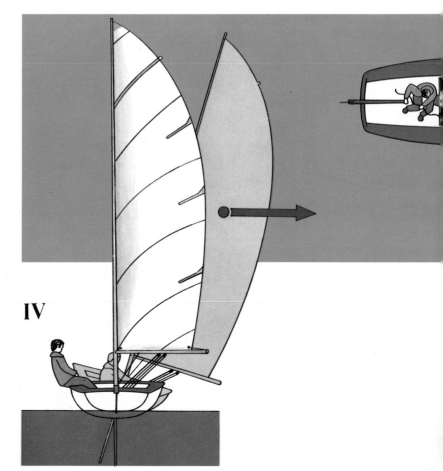

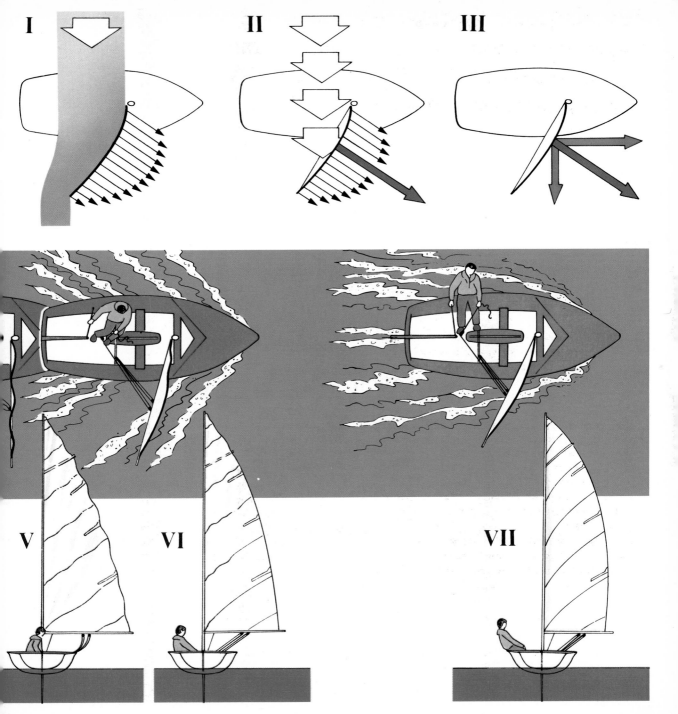

Steering a boat

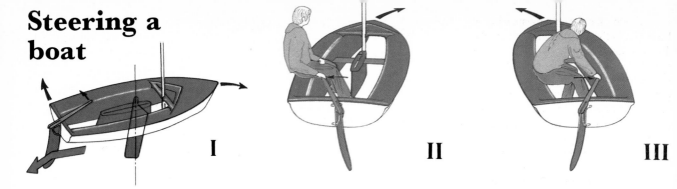

I   II   III

IV

V

VI

There is a knack to steering a boat just as there is to riding a bicycle. The two are similar in needing a sense of balance and a coordination of body movements. In Part One we explained that when the rudder blade is angled to one side the water flowing past it pushes the stern of the boat sideways and the bow of the boat is turned in the opposite direction (I).

The helmsman will normally sit on the windward side of the boat to have a good view of the sails and the course and should sit far enough forwards to be clear of the end of the tiller. When seated in this position you will find that if you pull the tiller towards you (II) the stern will move towards you and the bow will move away. Similarly, if you push the tiller away from you (III) the stern will move away and the bow will swing towards you.

In order to allow you to stay sitting on the sidedeck but still be able to control the tiller it is normal to use a tiller extension which is attached to the end of the tiller by a universal joint that allows the extension to be pivoted in any direction. In light weather the use of the tiller extension allows the helmsman to sit well forward where his weight is better positioned and still have full control over the tiller (IV, V, VI).

In stronger winds the helmsman sits further aft but must sit out to balance the boat and again the extension allows him to steer without changing his position. When sitting out (VII, VIII, IX) it is best to hold the extension in an underhand grip, while when sitting on the sidedeck or further forward an overhand grip is often more comfortable.

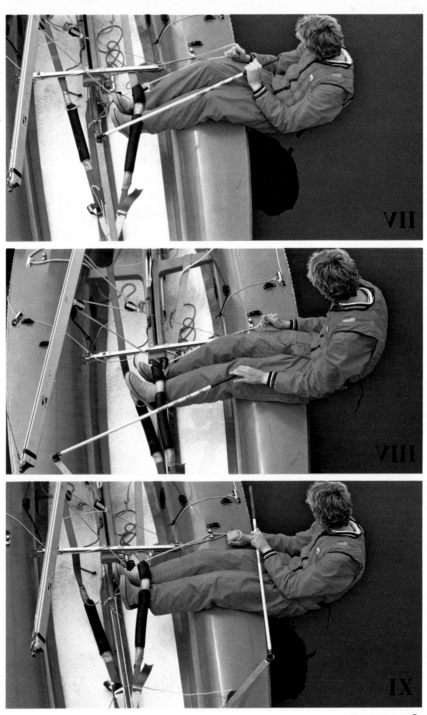

Steering for a mark

We have now seen how the boat can be made to accelerate and to slow down when the wind is from the side, or a-beam, and we have shown how the body weight is moved to counteract heeling, and have also shown how the boat is steered.

Your boat can now be aimed at a distant goal which is across the wind and be steered in that direction. In addition you can control the speed to some degree by easing the sails.

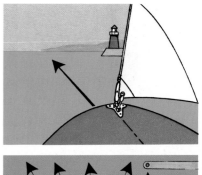

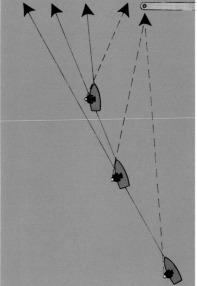

But there is another thing about steering which needs explanation. Unlike on a bicycle, the helmsman is not usually sitting on the centre line. In fact when sitting well outboard, his eye may be as much as six feet from the centre of a boat which is only 12 feet or so long. His eye is naturally attracted by the stemhead and the tendency is to line up the background with this and assume that this is the **course-made-good** by the boat. As can be seen this is not so, and the boat will either end up way to windward of its destination or will travel on a curved course.

Therefore, learn the knack of looking parallel to the centreline of your boat. It is the same sort of problem as trying to fire a pistol from the hip.

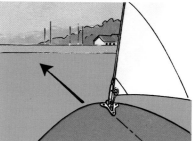

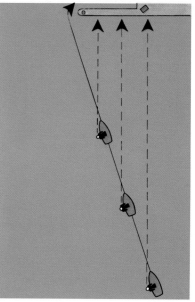

Orientation—the helmsman as a computer

The ideal way of learning sailing is by 'imprinting,' just like a baby learns to walk, but few of us are lucky enough to live in and around water to a degree that makes this possible. So we are here trying to convey by means of drawing and colour an indication of what a sailor has to learn to *feel*.

Sailing is not an exact science but more of an art. There are so many invisible forces of wind, wave and current to consider, so many variables to ponder and decide upon, so many small adjustments that can be made which have no precise measurement.

For example, the sailor may have to decide whether to sail a little closer to the wind direction to gain distance to windward at the expense of a slower boat speed—whether to aim off-course slightly to gain speed or to allow for the effect of a current—whether to slow down to avoid getting so much spray on board—whether to ease out the sails a fraction to reduce heeling and so relieve a tired crew and restore balance. And so on.

We have already introduced the idea of *seeing the wind*. Now we want to extend this to make use of more of the senses. The helmsman must be a computer which accepts all sorts of information and translates it first into a mental picture of the whole situation — orientation — and then comes up with one or more different alternative actions to choose from.

*The *eyes* are the most important receiver of data and should continually flick around to watch the waves, the goal, the flag, and luff of the sail, the positions of moving objects such as other boats or of fixed obstructions so that a mental map is continually being updated.

*The *ears* listen for the variable sound of the wind and also the noise of water at the bow indicating speed.

*The *face* and *neck* are sensitive detectors of wind speed and direction.

*The pivoting of the *body* detects the angle of heel, and hence wind pressures on the sails, whilst the *hand* feels the forces on the hull and water via tiller and rudder.

All of this information is used by a sailor.

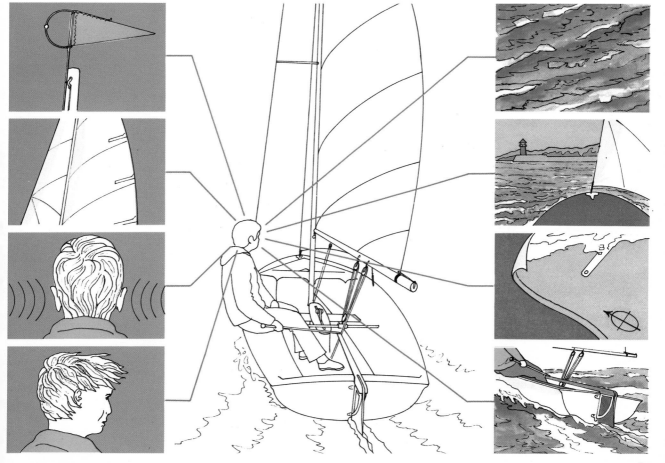

Luffing from a wind-abeam course

Changing direction more towards the wind is called **luffing.** The boats in these three sets of drawings are all luffing. In the left-hand drawing two things have been done wrong—the boat has been turned without the sails having been adjusted to the new relative wind direction and the crew's body weight is too far outboard to match the reduced heeling force.

In fact, as we shall explain later, you can expect a *greater* heeling force as you sail the boat closer to the wind's direction, but this is only true if the sail is adjusted to have *smooth* air-flow on the new course. In the second set of drawings we can see that this has been done, but the crew's weight is now not far enough outboard to match the new heeling force.

So the right way to luff, and at the same time maintain speed, is to sheet in the sails progressively as you turn and at the same time move your body outboard to restore balance, as in the right-hand group.

Another way of slowing down

The left-hand drawings do, however, show an alternative way of slowing the boat but it cannot remain like this for long since the wind will start to push it astern through the air resistance of the rig and hull. You can slow or stop temporarily this way and, because of the wind resistance, it is quicker in its effect than simply letting out the sails.

Bearing away from a wind-abeam course

Changing direction more away from the wind is called **bearing away.**

For the present we shall only go as far as a point where we can still maintain *smooth* air-flow over the sail. This means the point where the correctly adjusted sail comes up against the lee shroud and cannot be let out further.

So, from a beam-wind course, which is usually known as a **reaching course,** or a **reach,** we can bear away towards a **broad reach.** On the previous page the boat was turned from a reach to a **close reach.**

In the upper drawings the sails have not been eased out and the heeling force increases—the boat heels—and, incidentally, the sail will probably stall so that the total driving force will be reduced.

So to maintain balance and speed, the sail is eased out as the boat turns. In this case the heeling force will start *decreasing* due to the more favourable angle of the sail for forward push, and so the crew must be ready to move *inboard* as the boat turns.

Also, due to the more favourable sail angle the boat speed will normally increase. Reaching and broad reaching are the fastest points of sailing.

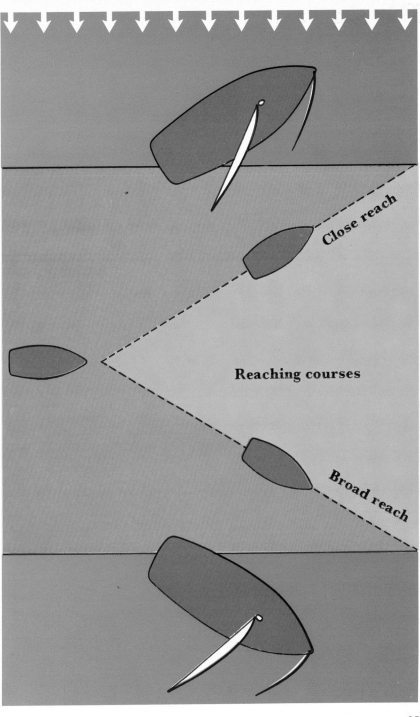

Close reach

Reaching courses

Broad reach

A

B

Using the toestraps and the tiller extension

Toestraps are essential if the crew are to be able fully to use their weight to balance the boat. They should be attached to the floor of the boat directly under the position of the feet when sitting out and should have high enough loops to allow the crew to sit out fully. Fit them so that your instep falls naturally under the loop.

The tiller extension should be long enough so that you can still push the tiller all the way to leeward when you are sitting out without you having to lean inboard.

The helmsman and crew work together

The helmsman's main job is to control the tiller at all times, hence the swivelling tiller extension (A). Secondly he controls the main-sheet so this must lead freely to either side (B). Additionally he adjusts the traveller and so the control lines and cleats are dupli-cated (C).

The Crew operates the centre-board which may have one control in the centre (D) or one on each side deck. But his main job is the jib sheeting which is duplicated together with its cleats (E). Addition-ally the crew deals with much extra gear such as the spinnaker, kicking strap, bailers, anchor and, of course, balance.

The helmsman and crew have a great number of things to do when working a boat. The helmsman how-ever, is not absolutely free in his movement since he must be able to see where the boat is going and he must be able to steer perfectly.

So the crew has to do extra balancing movements and may have to move over to the lee side at times so that the helmsman can remain in his commanding position.

The boat and its controls should therefore be so arranged that many of the important lines can be operated from either side when necessary.

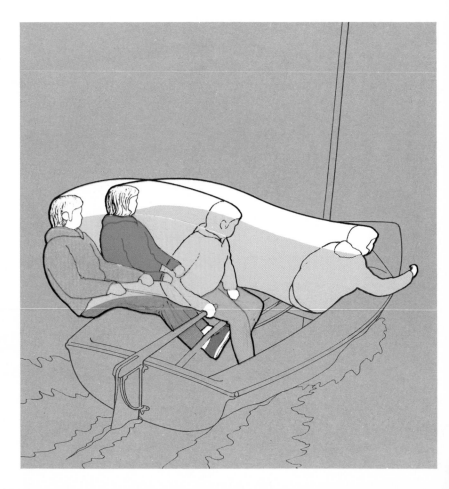

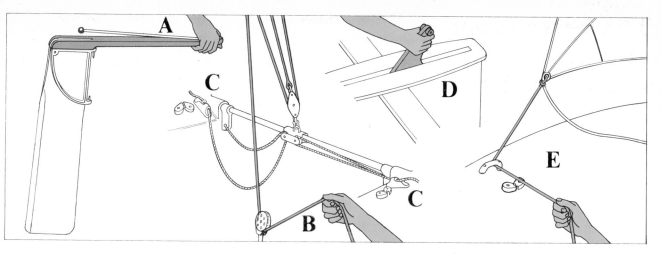

Mainsail and jib are adjusted together

It is best for beginners to start sailing with only one sail, the mainsail. Our early drawings in Part One started like this but very soon we were explaining about the extra power and better balance that can be obtained from any given sail area when broken into two parts. But to get these advantages it is necessary for the two sails to be worked together.

Again comes the essential knack of 'seeing the wind.' Without being able to visualize the air-flow a sailor can never hope to be able to adjust the sails perfectly. This is not to say that a boat cannot be sailed without this knack. Of course it can, but we see every day boats sailing with their sails incorrectly trimmed and thus not sailing perfectly, and to a true sailor such a sight is not a happy one.

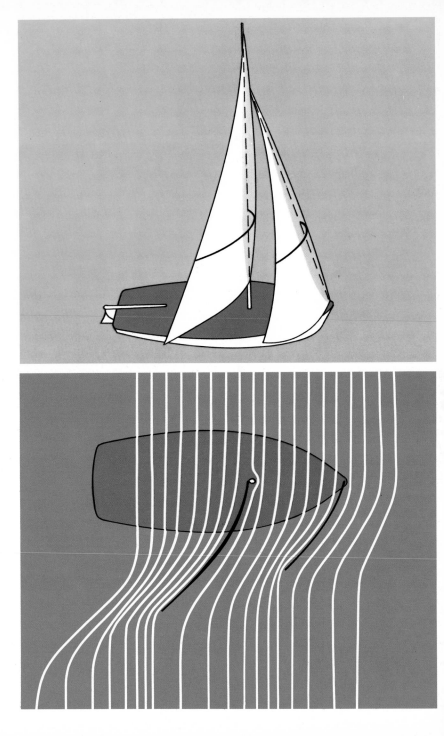

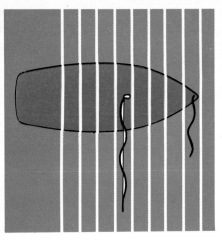 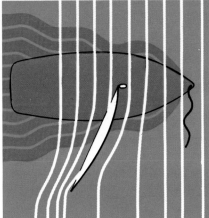 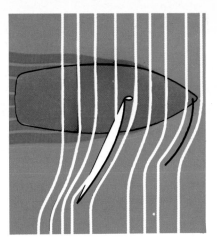

I. *Starting again from our beam-wind position. Both sails are flapping free, the air-flow lines are not diverted from their course and no power is developed.*

II. *Sheet in the mainsail and the boat heels and moves forward.*

III. *Sheet in the jib to establish smooth air-flow and the boat accelerates still more. The increased power is not only due to the extra sail area.*

IV. *Opposite, the sails are trimmed perfectly. Notice how the air-flow over the pressure side of the jib is diverted which not only produces a force on the jib but also helps the air-flow on the lee side of the mainsail to remain smoothly attached.*

V. *Below left and centre are the effects obtained when the jib is sheeted too close and when the mainsail is eased too much. The first is never right because it produces excessive heeling. The second is the way we* **spill** *power from our rig when overpressed or when we need to slow down.*

VI. *Below, two sails should normally be adjusted together at similar angles to the centre line. In practice the mainsail is always trimmed a little closer than the jib because you can see that it is working in air-flow that is already to some extent bent by the jib which is ahead of it.*

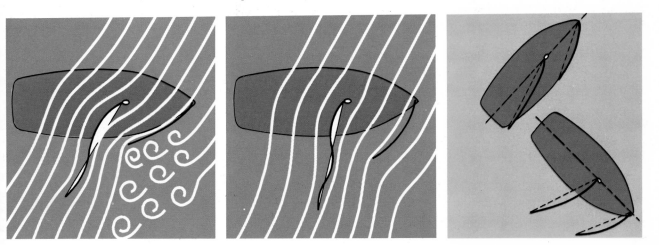

Sailing on a reaching course

So far we have mainly assumed that winds are steady in direction and strength. Some winds are but more usually they are constantly varying. In some places winds can be extremely unsteady and even violent. They can change in speed from nothing to 20 knots in seconds and just as quickly switch 180° in direction. Such winds are extremely difficult and dangerous to sail with.

Normally the fluctuations are only a few degrees in direction and perhaps four or five knots in strength in a twelve **knot** wind. One knot

is a speed of one nautical mile per hour.

For this reason you must always keep a sharp eye open to windward. **Gusts** or flat patches can often be seen by their effect on the water to windward and ahead. Changes in direction can be felt by the alterations in a boat's balance and can be seen on the burgee.

Study this drawing and notice the effects on the boat of a **shift** in the wind direction and then a gust, followed by a lull and a shift back

again—quite a common sequence. Notice the effects and how the crew correct the trim so that in 1, 3, 6 and 8 the boat is again in perfect balance.

1. *Beam wind. Boat in normal trim.*

2. *Wind shifts ahead. Sails lift and flap. Boat heels to windward.*

3. *Crew sheet in sails. Trim is restored.*

4. *Heavy gust. Boat heels over even though crew lean outboard.*

5. **Sheets eased.** *Boat comes upright. Crew start to move outboard and sheet in again.*

6. *Crew sitting fully out. Sails filling. Normal trim.*

7. *Wind shifts back and drops. Sail is stalled. Crew too far outboard. Boat heels to windward.*

8. *Ease sheets to establish smooth airflow. Crew sit on sidedeck—normal trim.*

Luffing to a close-hauled course

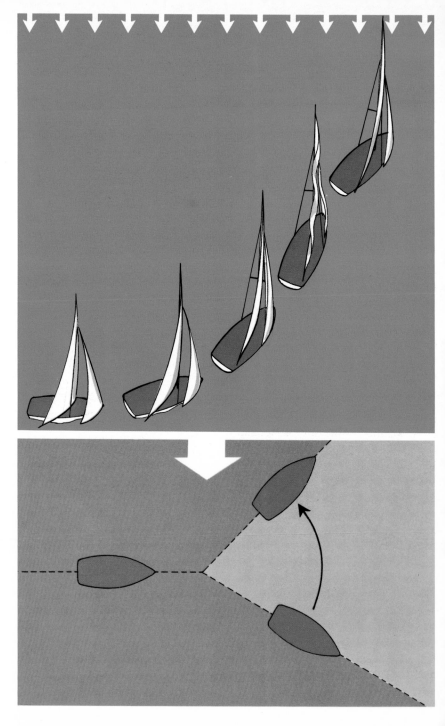

We have seen how we can 'luff,' that is alter course to sail closer to the wind's direction, and at the same time how we sheet in the sails as we luff in order to maintain the *smooth* air-flow that we need.

Eventually we shall reach a point where, if we alter course any closer to the wind, we cannot sheet in the sails any more. If we turn further the sails will start to lift at the luff and the boat will immediately slow down. We must hurriedly turn back a little until the sails fill again before the boat has slowed down to a halt.

If we make sure that we do not cross this invisible line then our range of possible courses can now be extended from a broad reach up to a **close-hauled** course.

As we turn so the two sails are steadily sheeted in together. Remember that the total force of a sail acts approximately at right angles to the chord of its curved section. Remember also, that, when we were beam reaching this force was favourable. Most of it pulled the boat along and only a small part of it caused the boat to heel.

When we sail close-hauled the direction of the force is not nearly so favourable. Not only is there a very small forward component but also the side force is greatly increased.

This means that the heeling effect is much greater and so extra crew weight on the side is needed. Also, the steering through waves and the attention to balance must be more accurate to make the most of this tiny forward pull.

One more thing; the wind speed will *feel* more since the boat is moving nearly into the wind and thus adds its speed to that of the wind. The sail forces are therefore greater still and the wind resistance of the boat becomes important.

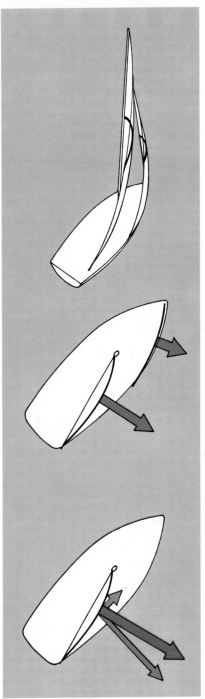

The centreboard— side-slip and heeling

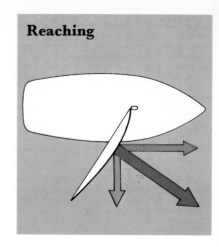

Reaching

We have already introduced the centreboard as an anti-side-slip device in Part One and you will by now be quite familiar with its working. The centreboard counteracts the force of the water when the wind is trying to push the boat sideways, but it is made thin and flat so that it has only a very low forward resistance. But another side effect of the centreboard is to increase heeling.

In a light dinghy the centreboard is usually made of wood and therefore does not aid stability as far as its weight is concerned. Instead, the water pressure against it *adds* to the wind's pressure on the sails to make the boat heel. When the crew move their body weights they are balancing both these forces (I–IV).

When a boat turns to a close-hauled course we have seen that the sideways component of the sail's force is greatly increased. Hence the tendency to side-slip is increased. And so it follows that the crew have to move their bodies outboard much farther to balance these increased forces (V–VIII).

Reaching. The side component is small. The water's resistance is low. The crew sit on the side deck.

Close-hauled. The side component is large. The water's resistance is large. The crew must get their weights outboard to balance the forces.

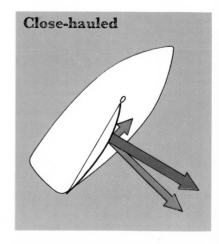

Close-hauled

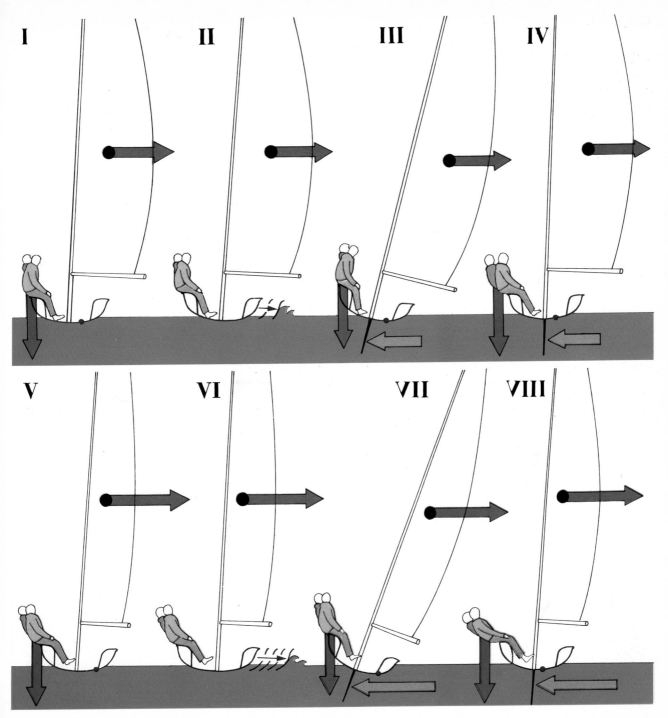

II

III

IV

V

VI

VII

VIII

Sailing on a close-hauled course

Sailing close-hauled means trying to gain as much distance to windward as possible as fast as possible. There is great skill in this part of sailing. Racing sailors are forever trying new adjustments to try to gain an extra few yards on a two mile windward course. It is a matter of boat tuning and also the fine balancing of several conflicting possibilities.

You can ease sheets slightly and sail faster but not so close to the wind. You can steer closer to the wind but accept a slower boat speed. Therefore, having selected your closest sheeting point it is then like sailing along an invisible line. You can luff over the line but then the power fails and you slow down. You turn back to the line and you pick up speed again.

You can also try sheeting your sails closer to the centre line (I). You can then sail closer to the wind and still keep them filled but the side force increases and the forward force decreases. If you continue you will reach a point where the forward force cannot overcome wind and wave resistance (II). Go further and you start to be pulled astern (III).

There is no avoiding the fact that for any given boat and suit of sails it cannot be made to sail to a windward goal any faster.

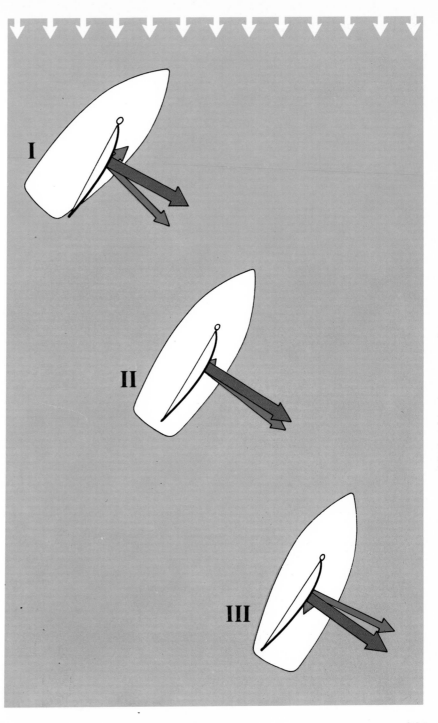

Following the fluctuations of the wind

The invisible line which you cannot profitably cross is not always straight. If the wind shifts then you may be able to alter course a little nearer your goal. This type of wind shift is called a **freeing shift.** You can then either sail on your existing course with sheets eased or **freed** a little or you are free to steer a little closer to a windward goal.

Alternately the wind might shift the other way and cause your sails to lift and flap. You are then said to be **headed** off your course. It is a **heading shift** and you must sail a little further away from your goal. The angle of the invisible line has in fact shifted round slightly against you.

Constantly watch for these slight shifts to get the best out of your boat.

Dealing with harder gusts

The wind also constantly varies in strength. A hard gust may cause you to heel excessively and yet you may already be sitting as far outboard as you can go. You are said to be **overpowered.**

There are two things you can do. You can luff a little more and let the sails lift and thus reduce power and heeling, but the boat will slow down quickly and so this is only a very temporary answer (A).

Better is to ease the mainsheet a little as the puff strikes you thus allowing the air-flow to spill off the sail and reduce power and heeling (B). Continual small movements in and out keep the boat in balance and maintain a good speed.

Except in extreme cases do not ease the jib since it can flog violently and increase its resistance without giving much extra forward drive. Better to keep it tight and flat.

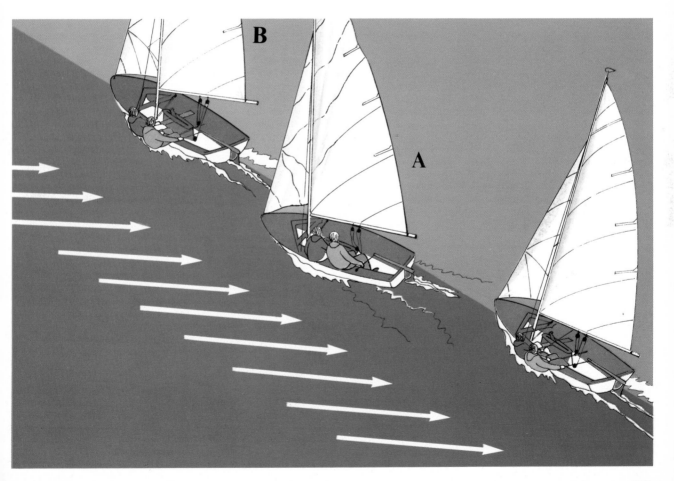

Luffing head-to-wind, stopping and going astern

We have already said that you can deliberately luff across the invisible line in order to slow down on purpose. You should now practise this because it is the important first part of several essential manoeuvres.

Start with a good speed, then luff head to wind and allow the boat to **shoot** straight into the wind with sails flapping. You will have to move inboard to keep the boat balanced.

Just before the boat stops dead, back the jib by pulling in the sheet that is on the windward side. This will blow the bow back onto course aided also by putting the tiller over. Then reset the jib on the correct side. The sails will now fill, and so you regain your positions on the side decks. The boat will accelerate and you will be under way again.

Using the first part of this manoeuvre — **shooting head to wind**—you can stop alongside a jetty or pick up a buoy but practice is needed to judge the speed of approach. You will shoot further in smoother water and lighter winds (I and II).

If you realize that you have under or over estimated the speed you can continue as before by **backing the jib** and bearing away.

If you leave this correction too late, the boat will stop (III) and the wind will start to blow the boat astern (IV). If this is likely to happen, carefully glance at fixed objects or even at bubbles or specks on the water to establish whether the boat is moving ahead or astern.

If the boat does move astern you must immediately reverse the tiller because the water flow will act on it in the opposite sense. The boat will then quickly turn onto its old course, the sails will fill and you will move ahead again (V). As soon as it starts to move ahead, revert to normal steering.

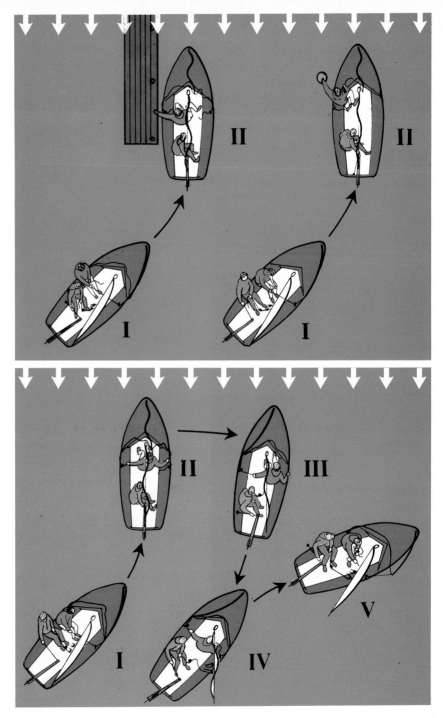

Port and starboard tacks

It will be clear now that we could just as easily have explained how to sail as far as this stage with the boat facing the opposite way with regard to the wind.

When a boat is sailing with the wind blowing over the port side it is said to be on **port tack.** With the wind coming over the starboard side it would have been on **starboard tack.**

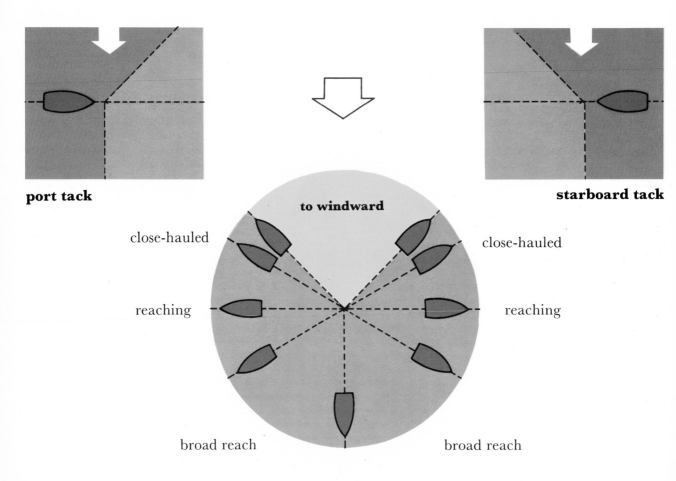

port tack

starboard tack

to windward

close-hauled

close-hauled

reaching

reaching

broad reach

broad reach

Changing tacks—the windward way

There are two ways of getting the boat from one **tack** to the other. Here is the windward way which we call **changing tacks** or more simply, **tacking.**

The first part is exactly the same as shooting head to wind. Then, instead of turning back onto the old tack, we simply continue to turn.

This means of course that the boom and sails swing flapping across to the other side until stopped on that side by the sheets whereupon the sails fill with wind on the new tack. At the same time both crew must change positions to the opposite side in order to restore balance.

So the principle of tacking is a logical development of all we have so far learnt. Now let us see how to do it in practice.

Tacking—the helmsman's actions

We show two different methods. The top row is for boats with central mainsheets or with the final sheet lead taken from in front of the helmsman. The lower row is for mainsheets led from aft.

I. With the boat having good speed push the tiller to leeward and ease the mainsheet slightly. As the boom moves in over the quarter move in towards the middle.

I. Push the tiller to leeward and move into the middle when the boom crosses the quarter.

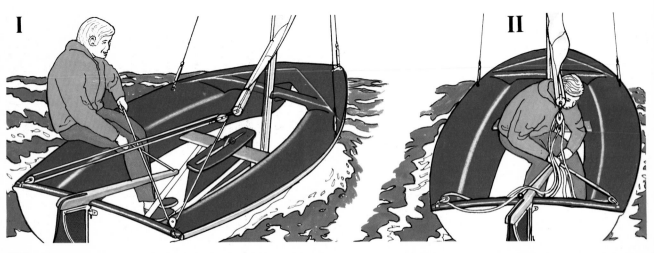

II. Step across the centre line and turn facing forward. Slide the hand down the extension and fold this aft holding the tiller behind the back.

III. Sit down and with the other hand still holding the sheet, catch the tiller and rapidly change hands on tiller and sheet.

IV. Sit out properly and adjust the sheet and tiller.

II. Step across the centre line and turn facing aft. Slide the hand down the extension and fold this aft.

III. Catch the tiller with the other hand. Turn and sit down.

IV. The forward hand takes the sheet. The other extends the extension. Sit properly and adjust tiller and sheet.

V   VI

Tacking—the crew's actions

After the command 'ready-about' and as the helmsman pushes the tiller to leewards (he will usually call 'lee-oh') the crew prepares to move into the middle as the boat come upright (I). She holds the jib sheet tight but picks up the new one as she moves (II). As the boat passes head to wind she frees the old jib sheet and sheets in the new one (III). As the boat turns onto the new tack she sits out to balance the boat (IV). The crew should usually move inboard, cross the boat and sit out on the other side before the helmsman although different helmsmen have their own preferences, of which the crew should be aware.

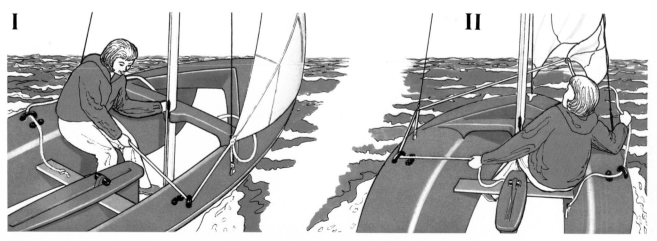

I   II

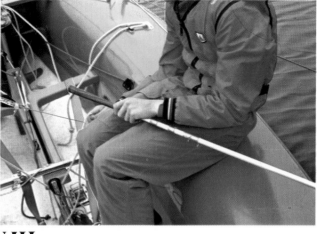

VII

VIII

Tacking—the helmsman's actions

The helmsman will usually evolve his own method for tacking but he should always aim to make the manoeuvre smooth. Long tiller extensions sometimes prove difficult but can be dealt with by practice. As the helmsman moves into the middle (V) he should retain hold of the extension with the old tiller hand.

When he sits down on the new side (VI) he will still be holding the extension in the same hand but with the hand behind his back. The other hand, still holding the mainsheet, now takes the extension and he lets go with the old hand. The extension is now in the correct hand (VII) and the other one takes the mainsheet so the helmsman can now sit out on the new side (VIII).

III

IV

Sailing to a windward goal

The diagram shows that we now know how to sail over a range of two arcs covering broad reaching to close-hauled on both tacks. We also know how to tack. Therefore, any point in the arc between close-hauled and head to wind can also be reached by sailing for appropriate distances on one tack and then the other.

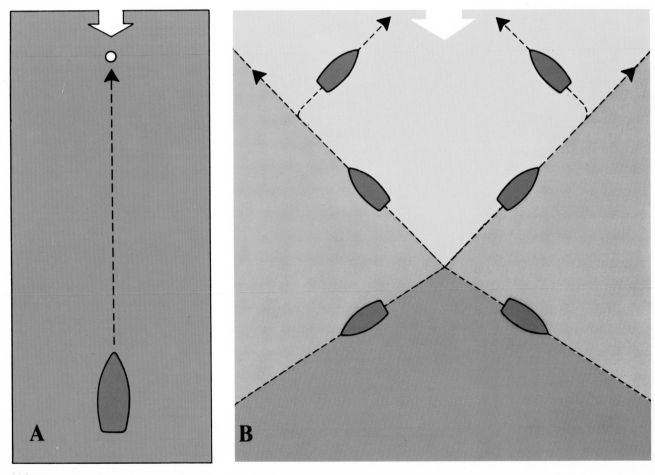

A

B

There are in fact an infinite number of ways of reaching any goal that is too far to windward to be arrived at on a single close-hauled course.

Thus on open water there is a wide choice of courses which can include one tack or many. Also, on restricted water, or where there are obstructions in the way, a choice of close-hauled courses interspersed with tacks at appropriate points can enable us to arrive at our goal.

We can work out with the aid of a mental map of the situation, the best way of reaching the goal using the safest course and the fewest tacks.

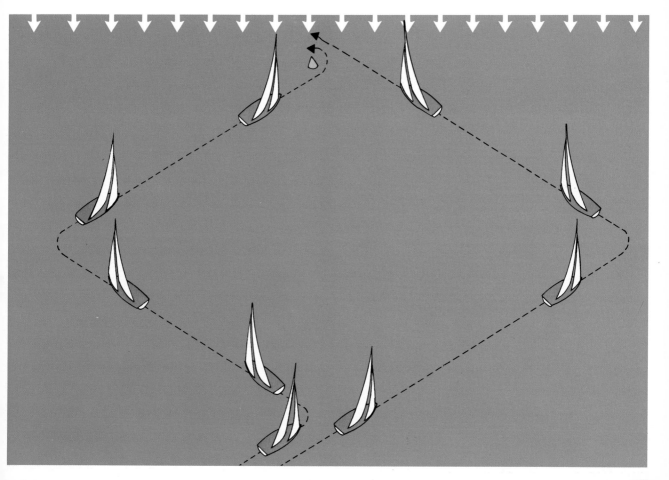

The effect of leeway on a windward course

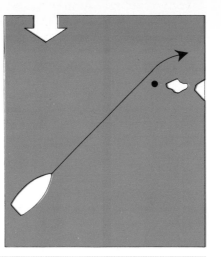

We said that the centreboard prevents side-slip, or **leeway.** Of course, it does not completely do so. There is still a small but appreciable amount of side-slip just as the centreboard also has a small amount of head resistance even though made thin and flat (I and II).

We also said that, when steering for a mark, you had to 'aim off' to allow for your eye being substantially away from the centreline.

Allowing for leeway is another of these adjustments which practice

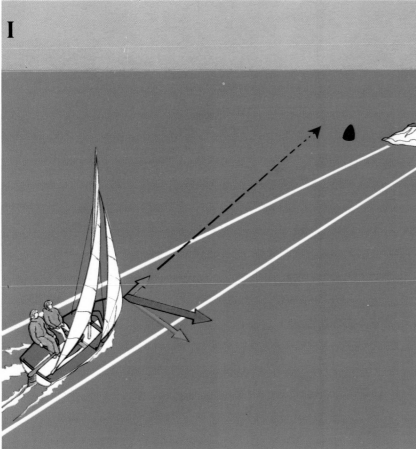

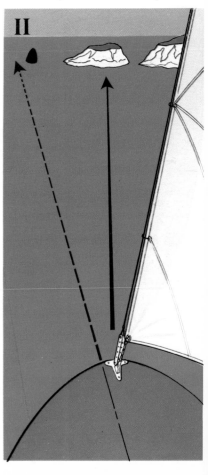

will enable you to do automatically. For now you simply need to realize that leeway is only important when you are sailing close-hauled and is rarely noticeable on a reach unless of course for some reason the centreboard is fully raised.

Also, to some extent the effect of leeway cancels out the effect of your eye being off the centreline. Therefore for practical purposes you will find that sighting just to windward of the forestay will approximate to your true course-made-good when sailing close-hauled.

Therefore if you aim the boat in the normal way when close-hauled, leeway will cause you to end up some distance leeward of your goal (III).

So, aim off a little to windward (IV) and the boat travels slightly crabwise towards the goal (V).

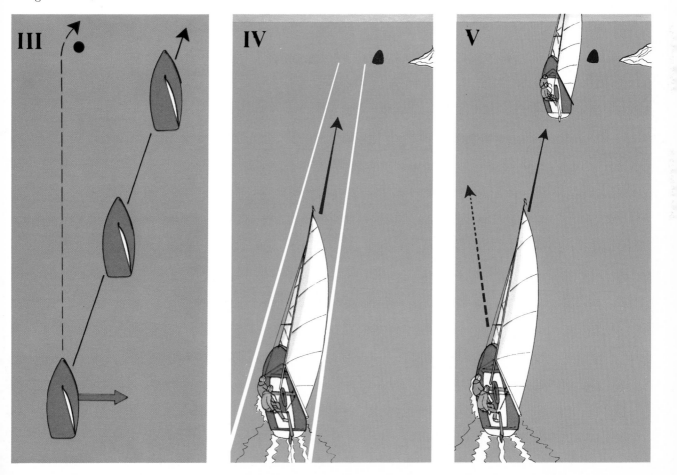

Avoiding collisions when close-hauled

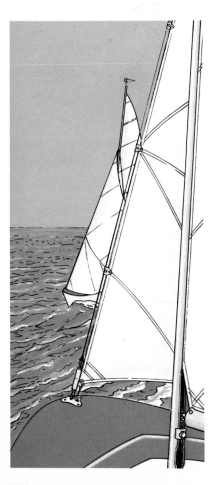

By now you should be getting quite good at estimating angles and distances. You may already have met and avoided obstructions and other moving objects.

If you suddenly see another approaching boat start to appear round the forestay, one or other of you must do something quickly or there will be a collision.

If the situation is as in the picture, our boat is on port tack and the other is on starboard. In Part One we said that *port* was *red* and *danger*. *Starboard* was *green* and *go ahead*.

We are on port tack and in danger. It is for us to get out of the way.

So now we have another use for two of our new skills. We have two options. The first is to bear away, so ease sheets in plenty of time and steer to pass clear of the other boat's stern (I).

The second alternative is for us to tack. So call 'lee-oh!' to the crew, put the tiller a-lee in plenty of time and tack before you endanger the other boat (II).

The starboard tack boat should hold her course to avoid confusion and hail 'starboard' to warn the port tack boat.

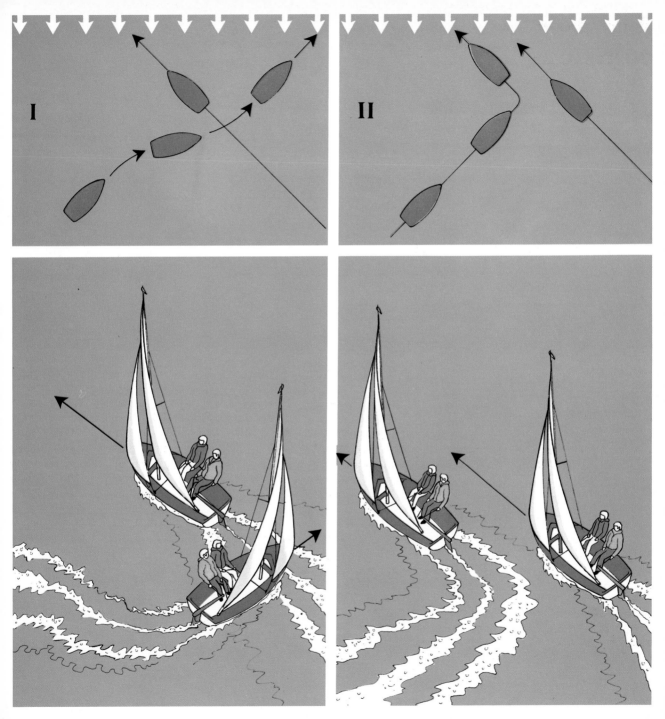

Right-of-way rules

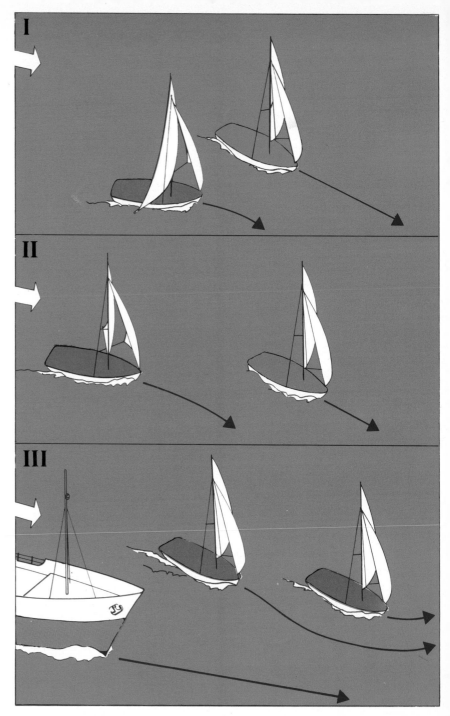

I. We have seen that a boat close-hauled on *port tack* has to keep clear of a boat on starboard tack.

This is true for all points of sailing and so a boat running on *port tack* keeps clear of a boat on starboard tack whether close-hauled or running or any course in between.

The other important basic rules are as follows:

II. When both boats have the wind on the same side, the *windward boat* keeps clear.

When one boat is overtaking another it is the *overtaking boat* which keeps clear.

III. Though, on open water, a boat under power gives way to sail, in practice this almost *never* happens to a small sailing boat because, in channels or harbour limits, larger craft even when powered have to be given room since their manoeuvrability is restricted.

Bearing away to a wind-astern course

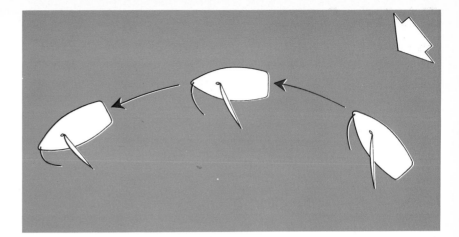

We have reached our windward goal. We now want to return straight before the wind.

We can bear away, easing sails to the point where the boom touches the shroud and then turn still more until the burgee says that the wind is coming from right aft.

Sail forces on a wind-astern course

Sailing with the wind astern is very different from sailing close-hauled.

We have continually emphasised the importance of maintaining a *smooth* air-flow over the sails. Sheeting in causes the sails to stall and the flow becomes turbulent on the lee side. The power of the sail drops quite suddenly.

With the wind astern the boat is being carried along by it and the sail is stalled. The sail is not producing power at an angle to the wind's direction as it does when the air-flow blows across its surface. Instead it is catching the wind in an amount related to its area and this weight of wind produces a force which pushes it forward.

The wind fills the sail and spills off all round its edges. Such small side force as there is only results from the mechanical limitations of the rigging which cannot allow the boom to be squared off completely.

The centreboard can be almost completely raised, only the tip being needed to provide a little extra grip to aid steering.

The crew have to sit on both sides of the boat since there is almost no side force to balance.

Apparent wind strength

When sailing close-hauled most of the speed of the boat can be added to the wind speed to arrive at the real speed of the air-flow over the sail. This is called the 'apparent wind speed'.

With the wind astern the speed of the boat should be subtracted to get the apparent speed.

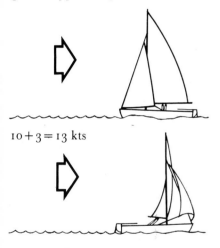

10 + 3 = 13 kts

10 − 3 = 7 kts

Typical values for a small boat show that the apparent speed can be halved as the boat bears away and at the same time the sail stalls. So the power of the sail drops dramatically.

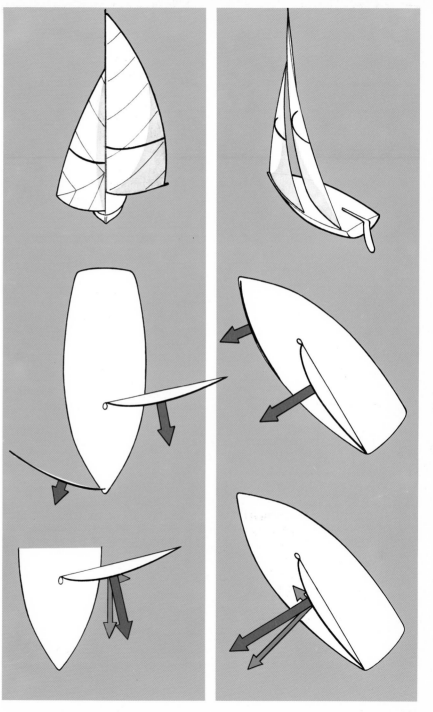

Sudden changes in trim and balance

I

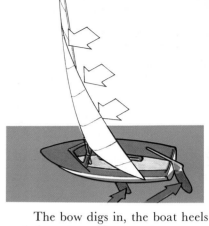

II

When the boat bears away from a close-hauled course to a course with the wind aft we have seen that the forces change considerably.

If we bear away slowly and steadily we have time to adjust the trim of the sails and to move our weights to keep the boat in balance.

We have to ease out the sheets and at the same time pull the tiller to windward, and raise the centreboard. As the boat bears away more, sheet has to be eased out progressively and the crew must smartly move inboard.

Especially at the beginning of this manoeuvre there are many things to do all at once. If you turn too quickly the forces very suddenly switch round and it is easy to be thrown severely off balance. In a fresh wind and with a light powerful boat, this is the most likely place where a capsize can occur.

At the beginning of the turn if the sail is not eased the side force increases and causes excessive heel (I) rudder pressure increases trying to lift the stern and depress the bow. This severe imbalance is made worse by the side pressures on the centreboard (II).

If you ease the sheet too far too fast and at the same time turn quickly, there may not be time for the crew to move their weights inboard (IV). The boat heels to windward, centrifugal force pulls the mast outwards

The bow digs in, the boat heels and slows down. In an extreme case the boom end catches in the water and a capsize can result."

(V), but the final disaster is caused by sail twist (VI). The top of the sail sags ahead of the mast and the wind acting on it pulls the top of the mast irresistibly windward.

IV

V

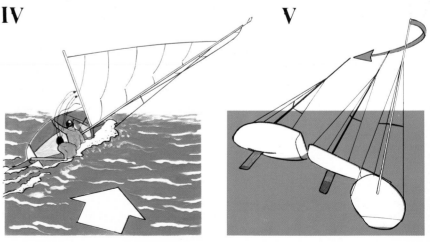

III

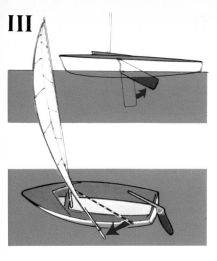

So ease the sheet and raise the centreboard part way before starting to turn (III).

The remedy, even in the final stages, is rapidly to sheet in the mainsail a little way.

VI

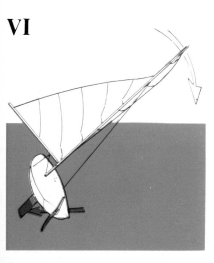

Running before the wind

This wind-astern course is known as **running** before the wind. The boat is 'on a run'.

Once the problems of the change of trim have been mastered, a running course becomes a relatively quiet experience owing to the lower apparent wind speed and the lack of need for balancing severe heeling forces. The crew can relax somewhat and the helmsman only has to concentrate on steering.

Indeed, the steering on a run is really rather important and the helmsman should not be lulled into a false sense of security by the quiet and relaxing feeling. Keep watch on the burgee and on the waves to make sure that the boat does not wander off course.

Luffing will result in a rapid increase in speed and heeling. Bearing away will end in an unexpected and sudden **gybe** which we shall consider next.

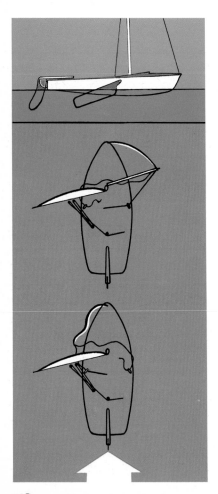

Our range of courses now nearly covers a full circle. We only need to know how to change tacks the downwind way to enable our boat to travel to any point we desire. On a run the mainsail will tend to blanket the jib which alternately hangs slack or fills. To keep it full of wind and to help balance the pressure of the mainsail the jib can be 'goosewinged' or set on the windward side. If the helmsman steers straight downwind this can be done simply by pulling on the windward sheet but it is better to use a 'whisker pole' which hooks onto an eye on the mast and the clew of the jib.

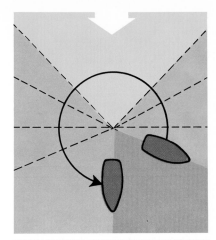

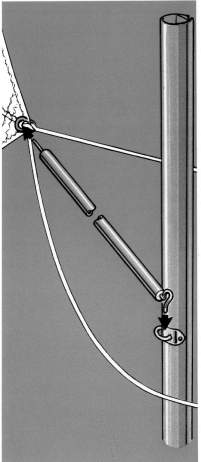

The principle
of a gybe

We have seen how we change tacks the windward way—that is by steering more towards the wind and making the bow pass 'through the eye of the wind'.

Gybing is accomplished by steering away from the wind till the stern passes through the wind's direction, (A and B).

When changing tacks, the essential thing is for the sails to move from one side to the other. The boat turns so that the wind blows over the other side. The sails being freely hinged to the mast, cannot stay on the old side and so they blow across (C).

So when tacking the sails first flap freely and then swing gradually as the boat turns until they are stopped by the sheets (D and E).

When gybing, the wind eventually gets behind the leach of the sail and quite suddenly blows the sail across in one violent sweep. It is this suddenness that makes gybing seem so alarming to the beginner.

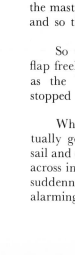

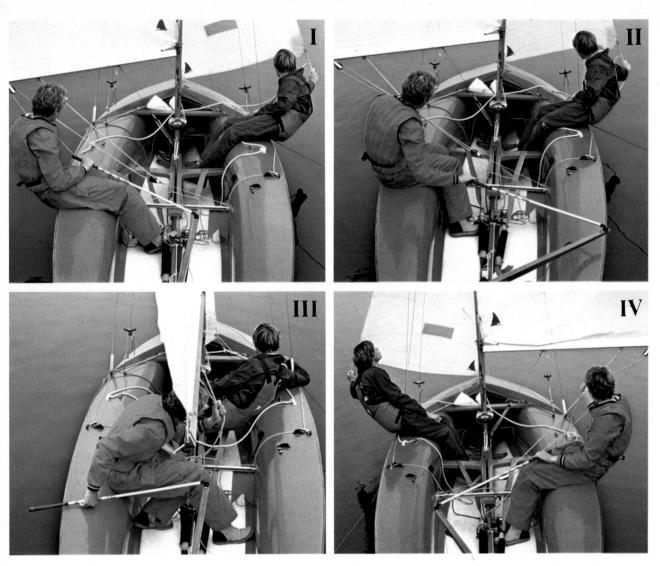

Gybing at its simplest consists of the helmsman turning the boat more and more to leeward (I and II). Eventually the wind gets behind the sail and blows it across (III). The helmsman ducks and moves across to the new windward side (IV).

Gybing from a run to a reach

The simple sequence just described is quite safe but not very satisfactory since the boat ends up stopped and there is a period just before the gybe when the boat is not properly balanced.

Co-ordination between helmsman and crew can improve control, make the gybe safer and more predictable, and also enable speed to be maintained.

Helmsman:

The boat here has the mainsheet led from forward of the helmsman. The lead of the sheet normally governs whether the helmsman turns facing forward or facing aft both when gybing and when tacking.

The Crew:

The crew's action in grasping the boom and heaving it across at the right moment is vital to the neat execution of the gybe.

The jib is not so important and, as long as the jib stick is removed, it

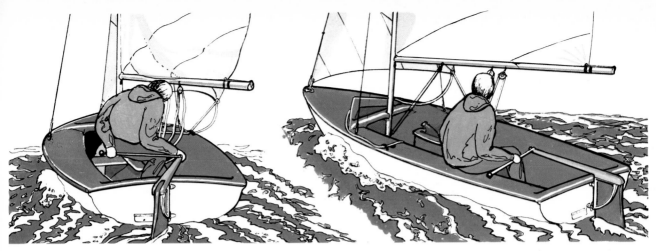

Here the helmsman pulls the tiller towards him folding the extension aft (I). In fact, if the wind is strong, he may put the extension to leeward so that it is ready placed for him to sit right outboard immediately after the gybe.

He starts to move across crouching low and pulls his sheet hand back to grasp the tiller behind him as he turns (II).

Then he turns and sits tucking his feet under the straps. His old tiller hand is behind his back and

rapidly moves to pick up the sheet which is still being gripped by the other hand on the tiller (III). He finally balances the boat and trims the sheet (IV).

---

can then be left free until after the main boom goes across.

The helmsman puts the tiller over and then calls 'gybe-oh!' This is the signal for the crew to grip the boom or kicking-strap firmly (I) and pull the boom over without hesitation

(II and III). Any delay or fluffing of this may easily throw the boat off balance and lead to a capsize. It is better for the crew to be over enthusiastic than to risk missing the right moment.

The crew then uses her weight to balance the boat and trims the jib (IV).

Picking up a buoy or floating object

Although a boat can be stopped by putting it head to wind—assuming there is no tide—it takes a lot of skill to be able to pick up a buoy or floating object by using this method. It is usually far easier and better to stop the boat in the required position by approaching on a close reach and letting out the sails to slow down and stop. In this way the speed can be controlled by easing sheets or by sheeting in and there is no danger of the boat getting caught in irons or tacking accidentally. This method also allows the crew to pick up the buoy or object over the side ahead of the shrouds rather than over the bow which is more difficult.

I. Stop the boat on a close reach with the buoy alongside the windward shroud so the crew can grab it. Make sure that the main and jib sheets are slack and raise the centreboard all the way up (A).

Pass the painter through the ring of the buoy and secure the end to the mast (B). Then it can be let go very simply without going forward (C).

I

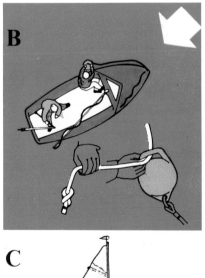

II. In tidal waters the current adds further complications. In a weather-going current, lower the mainsail and reach towards the buoy under the jib only.

Spill wind as necessary to control the speed and when the buoy is in hand raise the centreboard and lower the jib. Getting away again is the reverse.

III. Picking up a swimmer in a light dinghy can be tricky and the standard text book procedure for heavier boats does not always work.

If it is the crew who has fallen overboard, leave the jib to flap free. Using the mainsail get the boat level with the swimmer across the wind and slowly come towards her. Luff round her and ease the main sheet, stopping alongside and to leeward (a).

The swimmer can grasp the shroud and the thwart whilst the helmsman helps, keeping hold of the tiller with one hand (b). If the swimmer needs more help, let go the tiller and move forward to the shroud. Grasp the swimmer under the armpits, rock the boat towards her and use the buoyancy of the boat to help pull her aboard.

Don't come to windward of the swimmer since the boat will drift on to her and also the helmsman is unable to help without danger of a capsize.

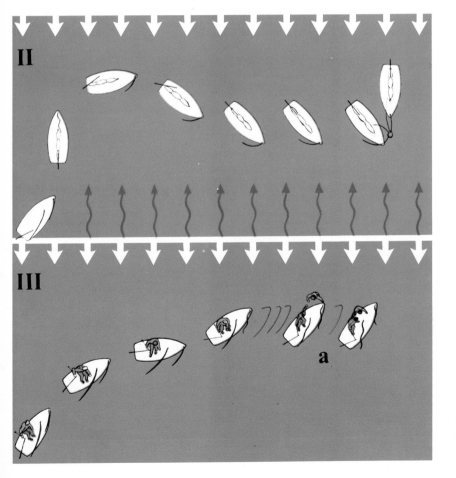

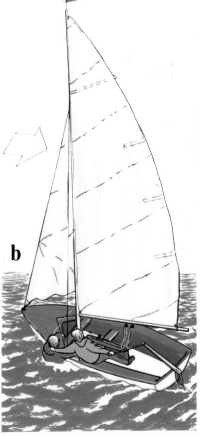

Sailing onto a beach

We show here a beach which is a lee shore since this is the most difficult both for landing and getting away. A weather shore will have calm water and you simply sail in with partly raised centreboard until it is shallow enough to jump out.

On a lee shore there will be waves and swell. When a suitable distance off put the boat head to wind, lower and lash the mainsail (a) and raise the centreboard (b).

Partly lift the rudder blade, or, if of the fixed type, unship it and steer with a paddle (c).

Sail in under jib only and keep the boat exactly stern-on to the waves (d).

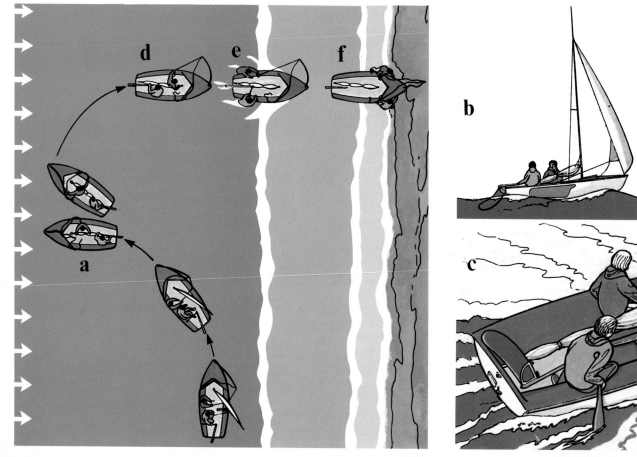

If there are big waves, get partly overboard ready to jump ashore (e) and, when the boat touches, very quickly run to the bow and pull it clear of the water (f).

If you are not quick the next wave will catch it and slew it round broadside. Apart from the danger of damaging the boat and rolling it on top of the crew it will also fill up with water and sand.

e

f

Sailing away from a beach

First establish if the wind is blowing directly onto the beach. If not, set the boat at the water's edge on the tack which will give the best angle of offing.

Rig the boat and hoist the mainsail. Either roll the jib or place it ready to hoist. Fit the lifting rudder

and prepare everything exactly so that there will be no hang-up or delay when starting to sail.

Pull the boat afloat. The helmsman gets aboard and lowers the centreboard and rudder as far as possible. The crew holds the boat head to wind.

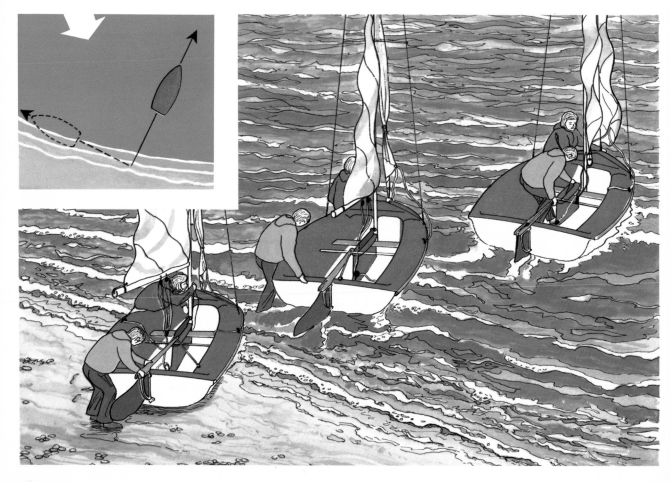

The helmsman sheets in the sail. The crew pushes the boat ahead and climbs in. The helmsman bears away and keeps the boat moving whilst the crew lowers the centreboard progressively as the water gets deeper.

Finally when deep water is reached, tidy up the boat and finish setting the sails.

If there is no lifting rudder, the boat will have to be sailed off with a paddle. The helmsman should use this to steer and also to push off the bottom whilst the crew balances the boat as well as working the mainsheet and centreboard. Be careful not to over sheet the mainsail or the boat may uncontrollably luff and then stop. You will be back on the beach before you realize it. When you are experienced you will be able to sail off a beach without a rudder by controlling the course using sail trim and crew position.

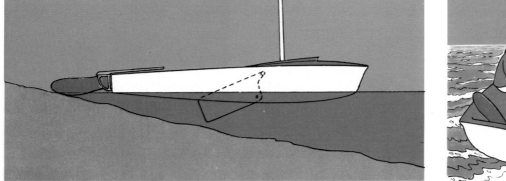

Arriving at a jetty or dock

We have already learnt all the essential skills necessary for making a safe landing at a harbour. Whichever direction is the wind we can arrange to arrive and stop either under full sail, one sail or with the paddle, which ever is appropriate.

If there is a current, make sure that you work out in advance, how it will affect your boat. It may work to your advantage by slowing down your approach. It may speed it up in which case you should allow more time to lower sails and slow the boat.

Remember the centreboard. Raise it to promote side-slip which may be helpful at times like this. Also remember to raise it as soon as you have made fast.

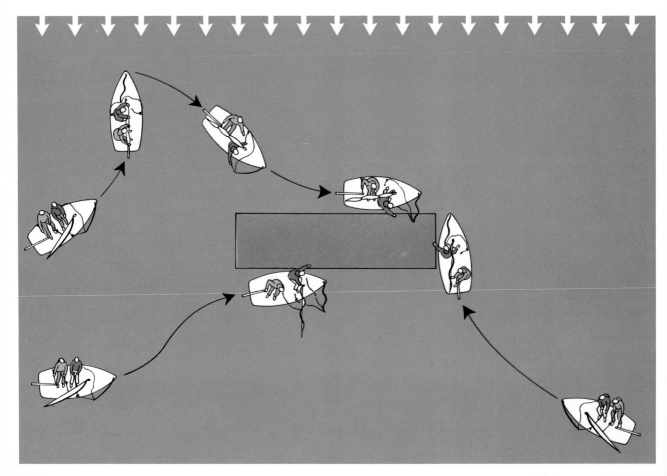

The same techniques are used for arriving at a jetty with mooring posts, but more careful preparation is needed in advance.

With a wind on the beam or astern it is best to lower the mainsail and to sail in slowly under jib only.

The helmsman should prepare a temporary stern line (which can be the mainsheet) with a big loop which can be thrown over the outer post as the boat comes in.

The best hitch for this loop is a **bowline** (pronounced *bō-lin*).

If the wind will be from dead ahead when entering the dock then the boat must be placed so that it can shoot the last few lengths with plenty of speed.

So leave all sails set and approach as near as possible on a reach. Only ease sails as you enter the dock. Be prepared to have the crew push out the boom to back the mainsail to stop the boat.

The helmsman should have a paddle ready for three reasons.

a) To help the boat reach the jetty if the speed was too low.
b) To act as a brake to stop the boat if speed was too great.
c) To paddle the stern to the mooring post after the crew has secured the bow.

When ready to leave it may be necessary to paddle clear if the wind is blowing onto the dock. If the wind is blowing off then you can drift clear or sail backwards by backing the mainsail.

Some more bends and hitches

We have shown in Part One some of the basic knots, bends and hitches used in mooring up and anchoring. Also the important bowline again on page 141. Here are a few more useful tips which are continued in Part Three.

Always have the possibility of being able to release anchoring or towing lines from aboard the boat. Use a **slip-hitch** (A).

Put anchor lines into a **fairlead** at the stem (B) or secure the line there with a loop of rope (C).

The anchor itself should be fastened with a **fisherman's bend** which is like a round turn and two half hitches but the first hitch is tucked behind the round turn to lock it securely (D).

The **painter** can be passed through a hole in the stem and secured to the mast heel (E).

The **reef-knot** (F) for tying two similar sized and lightly loaded lines can be freed easily by 'capsizing' one half with a sharp tug (G).

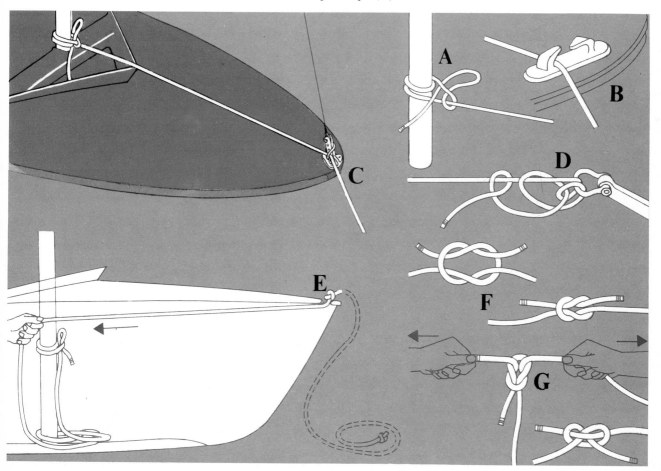

Three More Advanced Techniques

Contents

Picking up a tow

At the end of Part Two we left our boat moored or anchored. When a boat is anchored temporarily we say it is **kedged.** A kedge is any type of auxiliary anchor.

A kedged dinghy may be offered a tow by a motorboat. Or you may want to signal a friend for a tow. The universal signal is to hold up a rope's end or a coil of rope. Normally the towed boat should provide the towing warp.

A word of warning here—it is possible for the unwary to let them-selves in for a **salvage** claim. Basically, anyone who contributes to the safety of a boat or person who is in danger, and who acts voluntarily, can claim for salvage as long as all or part of the property is saved.

This would never apply in the case mentioned since you only have to wait for the current to ease or the wind to spring up or simply paddle ashore. But there may be times when you are in trouble and need a tow and so if one is offered and you are in doubt, it is as well to ask if salvage payment is required. Often the price

of a drink or of the extra fuel needed will be all that would be accepted.

The normal dinghy's painter is often quite useless for towing. Also, since it is fixed at the stemhead, there is no way of letting go in an emergency. If you have no other line which can be made fast round the mast you will have to accept the motorboat's warp.

Points to note:
When heaving a line, **coil** it fairly small, separate the coil into two parts and only heave one part letting the rest pay out from your other hand (A).

When under way, raise the centre-board and get your weight aft to raise the bow (B).

A motorboat's **warp** should have a loop in the end. Make a single (C) or double **sheet bend** (D) on the loop to fasten lines of dissimilar size.

Fasten the warp round your mast with a slip-hitch or simply take a turn round the mast and hold on to the end. Similarly tie a slip hitch to your mast or thwart if towing another boat (E).

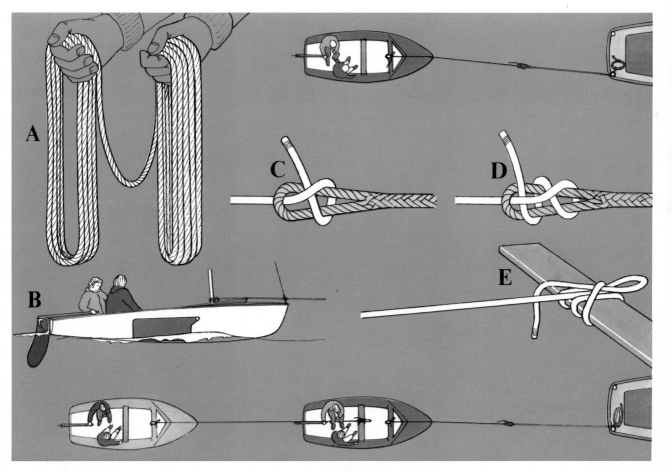

Towing problems

I. If you leave your centreboard down when under tow the boat will have too much grip on the water. It is necessary for the hull to be able to side-slip so that it can be pulled back on to course if it should wander. It may be impossible to get back into line behind a heavy motorboat even with the tiller over and the result will be a capsize and damage.

II. At the other extreme, a light speedboat or a dinghy with an out-board motor can easily be pulled right round by the towed boat. This often happens if the tow rope is fixed too far aft on the motor dinghy or is not taken via the stemhead of your boat but you can help by always aiming your boat at the point of tow.

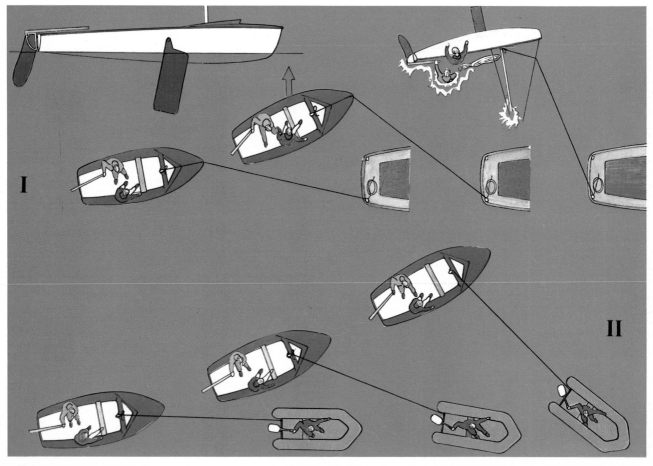

III. A properly organized tow for several boats is best done by first streaming a long heavy warp from the motorboat. The dinghies then pick up the warp at intervals and make their own lines fast to it with **rolling hitches.**

The rolling hitch consists of two turns round the warp followed by a half-hitch on the opposite side of the hauling part. Depending on which side the first two turns are made, so the hitch will be locked and will not slip along the warp in that direction (A). (See page 71.)

For safety use a slip-hitch on the last turn as shown. In this type of tow the painter should not be led through a bow fairlead or it will be impossible to keep the dinghy parallel to the tow rope.

IV. When a towing motorboat has to turn a corner, the golden rule, which is always to aim at the towing point, has to be relaxed somewhat. You have to imagine that you are on a railway track and follow round in succession.

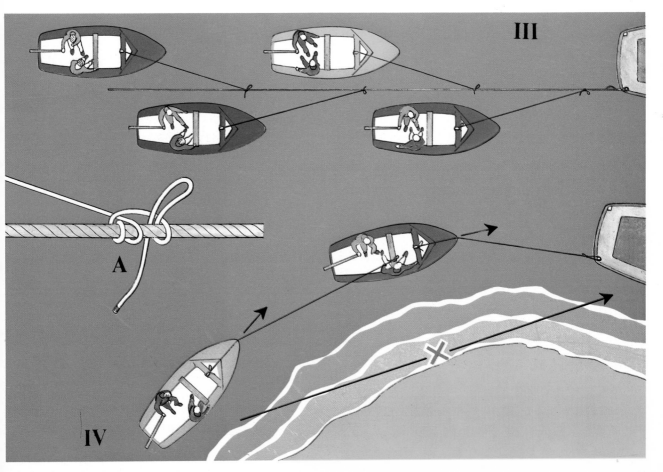

The spinnaker

With the wind from aft like this, the spinnaker is little more than a 'wind catcher.' It is made from very light cloth and is spread wide and deep to collect as much of the moving air-flow as possible so that the weight of air can push the boat along.

If there is any possibility of getting the air-flow to move across the surface rather than blowing straight into it then, like other sails, it should be trimmed accordingly to take advantage of the extra *pull* that the air-flow can generate.

The spinnaker is held steady from one corner by a rigid pole to the mast and is operated by a **guy** or **brace** on the pole and a sheet on the other free corner. It is symmetrical and so can be set on the other gybe simply by shifting the pole across.

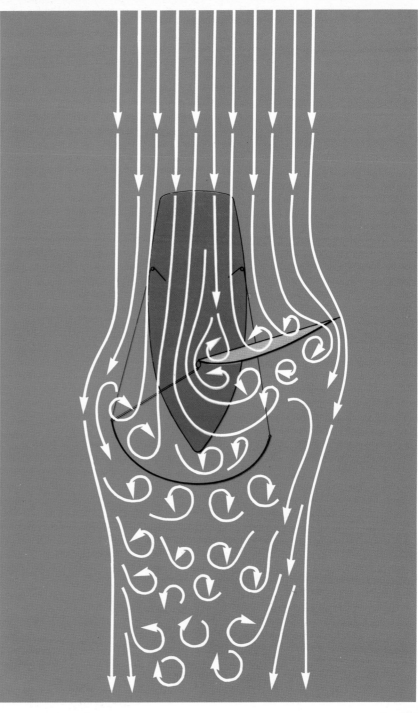

Preparing the spinnaker

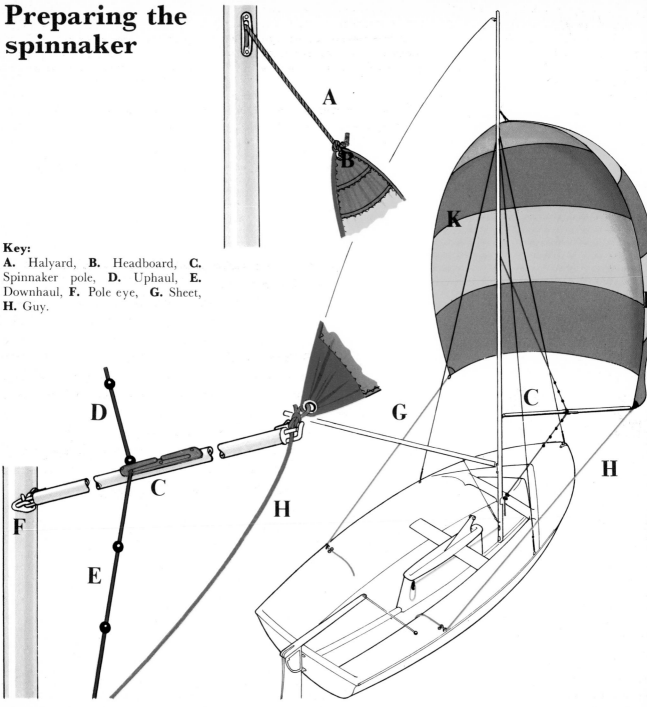

Key:
A. Halyard, **B.** Headboard, **C.** Spinnaker pole, **D.** Uphaul, **E.** Downhaul, **F.** Pole eye, **G.** Sheet, **H.** Guy.

The spinnaker being a large and baggy sail which is held rigidly at the top, semi-rigidly at the tack, and only restrained by the sheet at the clew, it can easily get out of control if not correctly managed. There is no mast or taut luff wire from which it can safely hinge and so it can flog violently when partially collapsed.

The drawing shows how the spinnaker control gear is arranged and the key gives the names of the parts.

The basic point to remember about the spinnaker and its gear is that the entire sail when set, together with its sheet and guy, is outside everything else. The pole is always on the windward side (opposite side to the main boom). The jib can be left set or rolled up or lowered as convenient and is not important compared with the spinnaker and mainsail.

It is often best to hoist to leeward since it will be blanketed by the mainsail as it goes up and will be less likely to fill with wind before you are ready and thus get out of control.

First flake it down carefully into its container or bag. Put the foot in first and lay the bottom corners out over the edge. Then feed in the rest making sure there are no twists by running your hand down one leach and then the other. Lay out the three corners on the appropriate side ready to connect the halyard and sheets.

The ends of the sheet, guy and halyard must all lead finally from outside the boat directly to the same point—the spinnaker container. If hoisting to leeward they all come in over the lee side—if hoisting to windward they all come in over the weather side.

Once they have been correctly led they can then all be clipped together at their ends and the whole group can be passed from the windward side to leeward side or vice versa by going round the forestay and they will still lead clear.

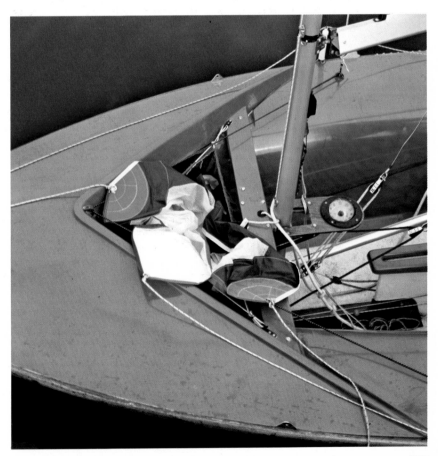

Hoisting the spinnaker on a run

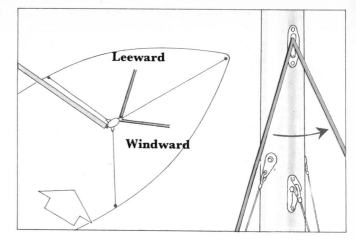

Leeward

Windward

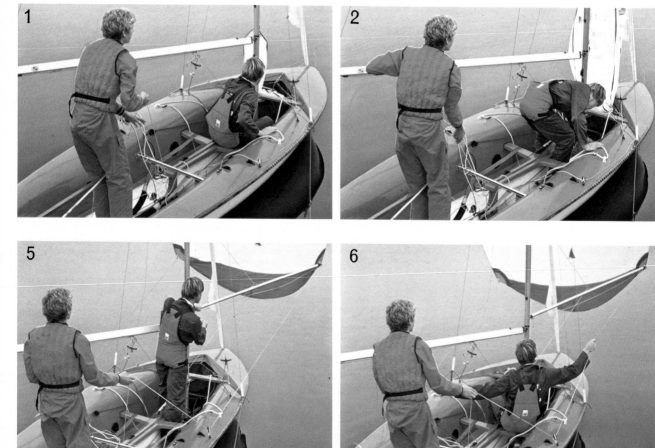

1

2

5

6

A spinnaker can be hoisted either to leeward or to windward depending on which side it has been rigged for hoisting. The leeward hoist is usually the easiest, especially for the beginner. The helmsman stands in the middle of the boat having put the boat onto a broad reach (1). He steers with the tiller between his knees (2) so that his hands are free. As the helmsman hoists the spinnaker the crew finds the pole, clips the outer end to the spinnaker guy (3) fits the uphaul and downhaul (4) and clips the inner end to the mast (5). As soon as the spinnaker is fully hoisted the helmsman cleats the halyard and trims the sail by pulling on the sheet and guy until the crew has finished setting the pole (6). The crew then takes the guy, adjusts and cleats it, before taking the sheet and trimming the sail (7). The crew sits where he can best see the sail and the helmsman then sits down to balance the boat (8).

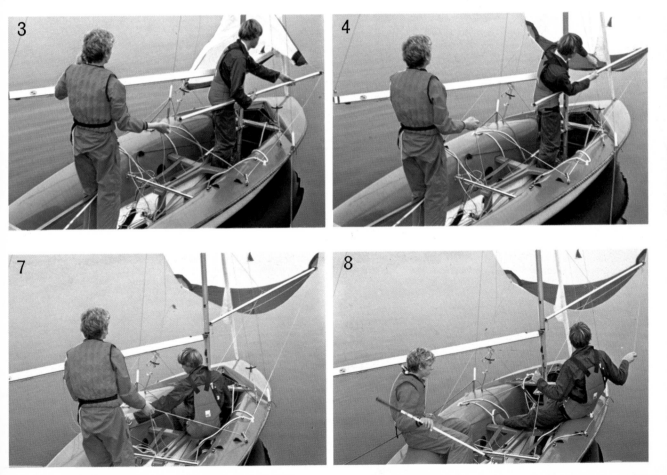

1

2

Hoisting on a reach

When it is necessary to hoist the spinnaker on a reach it is far easier if the spinnaker is hoisted to leeward or out of a spinnaker chute. This allows the crew to set the pole before the hoist so that the sail can be immediately brought under control (1).

As soon as the crew has connected the pole to the guy, up and downhaul (2), and the mast (3) the helmsman can hoist the sail (4). In medium winds or stronger, the helmsman will have to be able to hoist the sail while sitting out, in order to prevent the boat heeling.

While the helmsman hoists, the crew should pull on the guy to bring

5

6

the clew up to the end of the pole (5) then should roughly set the pole and cleat the guy (6).

With the guy and halliard cleated the sheet can be trimmed and crew weight adjusted to keep the boat level. Once the boat is settled on course the guy should be trimmed accurately to suit the apparent wind (7).

It is best if the crew sits or trapezes to windward in order to have a clear view of the spinnaker luff. If the wind is light the crew should not be huddled in the middle of the boat while the helmsman sits on the side deck. Instead the helmsman should move to leeward and leave the crew on the windward side deck or on the trapeze (8).

Reaching under spinnaker is one of the most difficult points of sailing. The closer to the wind the helmsman steers, the more critical is the spinnaker trim and the more the crew must concentrate. It is quite possible to carry the spinnaker too close with it trimmed in tight but the boat will feel sluggish. If it is not possible to bear away the sail should be dropped.

Reaching with a spinnaker

When running under spinnaker the boat is automatically in balance. The crew can sit on opposite sides of the boat and can correct any imbalance by adjusting the sheet or guy.

I. On a reach the pole has to be eased progressively forward and the clew has to be sheeted in. The major part of the sail's force will be sideways and so the crew have to get their weight well outboard.

It is a characteristic of spinnaker reaching that if speed can be kept up the boat will be easier to balance.

Once speed drops off, heeling force increases and it is hard to get moving again. You have to ease sheets and bear away and, when speed has been re-established, gradually edge closer to the wind to the point just before the speed falls again dramatically.

II. The spinnaker is a voracious feeder on air. It needs an enormous supply of new air to enable it to work properly, so speed is paramount. Never let the exit at the leach become strangled. Sheet in the mainsail.

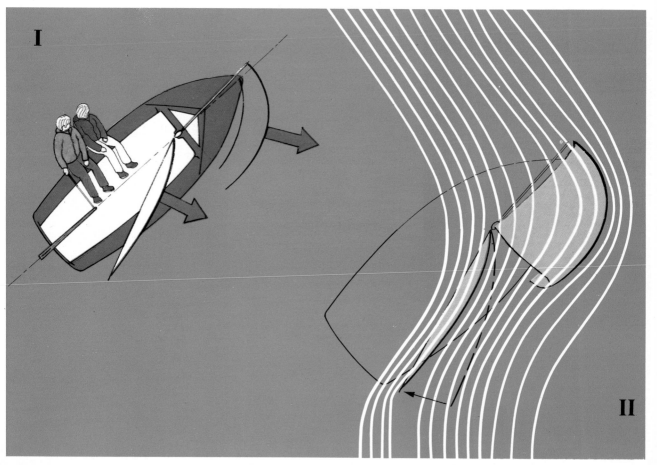

III. Keep the leach open (y) by every possible means. The pole can be set a little higher to get the 'ears' to drop away to leeward and to raise the sail. The sheet should be led to a point well aft to avoid pulling the leach in close to the mainsail. The guy is best dealt with by passing it under a reaching hook, with or without a cleat, by the windward shroud so that it is kept out of the way of the crew when they are trying to sit out or trapeze.

IV. Close reaching is the biggest problem and needs the greatest skill and most sensitive cooperation between helmsman and crew. The pole should be almost touching the forestay so that the luff of the sail can accept the wind at the most forward angle possible.

V. A really expert crew can do still more and perhaps squeeze another degree or two nearer to the wind. If the halyard is let go a foot or so the whole spinnaker drops to leeward and forward slightly. This will make 'y' larger and at the same time give a slightly improved angle of attack to the wind.

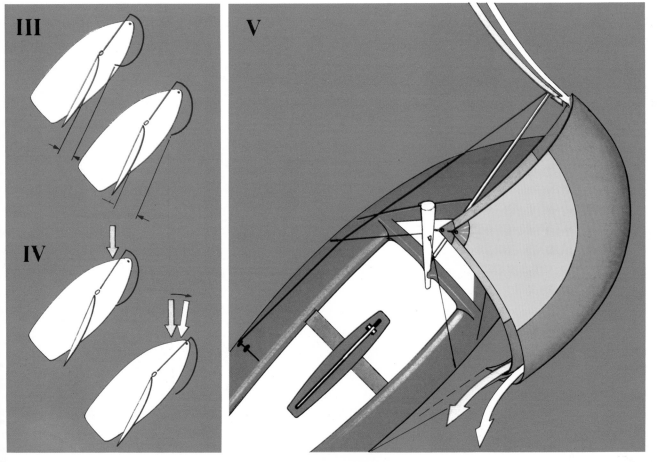

Basic spinnaker trimming

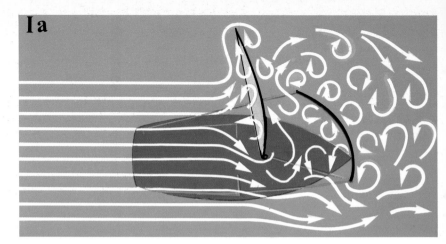

I a

The basic aims are to some extent conflicting. We need the maximum area exposed to the wind but we also want to encourage a flow of air across the surface.

I. Air-flow:

a) Sheeted in too tight. Wrong on both counts. Projected area is poor and the cross-flow is strangled.

b) Eased too much. The luff collapses very suddenly and the sail flogs violently.

c) Perfect trim. The sail is eased until just before the luff starts to curl in or 'break.'

II. Trimming technique:

a) The crew keeps a very close watch on the luff. The edge has started to curl.

b) The crew gives a very sharp jerk or tweak to the sheet. The sail makes a short arc anticlockwise and the luff curl flips back into place.

c) The crew immediately eases the sheet again slightly since it will have been overtrimmed by the tweak.

Good crews are able to keep a spinnaker just on the point of breaking by continual very slight tweaks followed by an immediate easing.

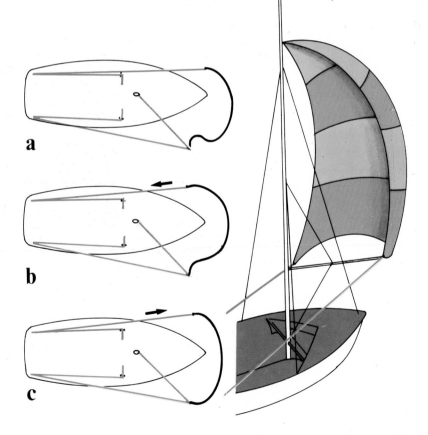

II

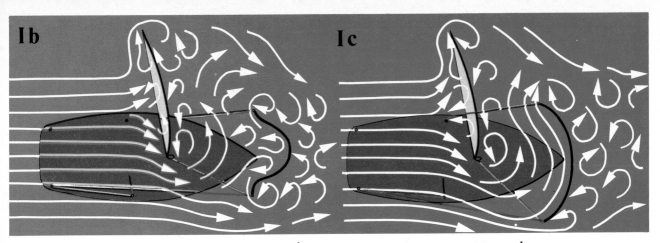

I b

I c

III a

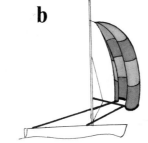

b

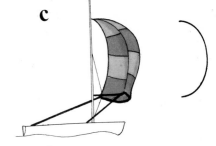

c

III. Pole height:

a) Pole set too high. The spinnaker goes flat and the **ears** collapse forwards. Power is lost. A hard weather technique.

b) Pole set too low draws the leaches too taught and they curl. The luff will 'break' too early.

c) Set to perfection, the clew and tack are nearly level and the cross-section is an even curve.

IV. Pole angle:

a) Too far aft. Projected area, 'x', is large but the important cross-flow is blocked because 'y' is so small.

b) Too far forward for a running course. Projected area is small. 'y' is large but the cross-section has too deep a curve for good cross-flow.

c) Pole about 45°. A good compromise and it is this angle for which the sail is designed.

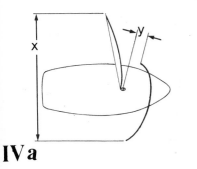

IV a

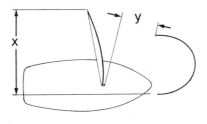

b

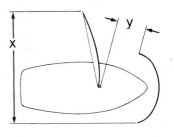

c

Spinnaker problems

I. The hour-glass:

A common problem especially when hoisting. Often caused by the spinnaker being packed into the container with twists in it. It can also be caused by slow hoisting. The sail then has time to flog about and wrap itself into this shape.

Hoist quickly and at the same time haul on the guy and sheet to keep the leaches apart.

II. The windward roll:

Ideally the driving forces of the spinnaker and mainsail when running should be so directed as to balance the boat. In an extra heavy gust the boat will then simply accelerate still remaining in balance.

If the sheet is eased too much or the pole is brought aft, the force will be directed too much to the side and, though the crew's weight can normally correct this imbalance, a gust may cause a violent windward lurch.

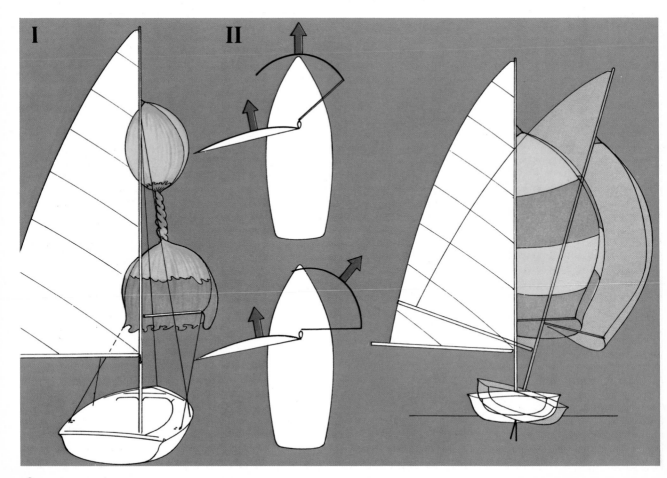

In a keel boat this will continue as a rhythmic roll but in a dinghy the first lurch can sometimes end in a capsize.

At the first sign of instability haul in the sheet smartly.

III. Broaching:

Usually this occurs when trying to reach as close as possible but it can also happen in a big sea if the boat is thrown violently off course by a wave. Also when the helmsman loses control during a gybe.

Broaching is an uncontrollable swing towards the wind. It ends with the boat lying well over to leeward with the sails flogging or can result in a capsize.

The direct causes of the common close-reaching broach under spin-naker are excessive sideways and forwards force from the spinnaker coupled with excessive heel. The rudder comes partially out of the water and the boat pivots on its lee-side, the mast being pulled round in an arc by the spinnaker's force.

To prevent a broach the boat must be held upright. There is then little or no turning effect. If heeling starts it must be resisted by getting the crew's weight outboard, bearing away slightly and easing sheets. The centreboard also should be about one half to two-thirds raised.

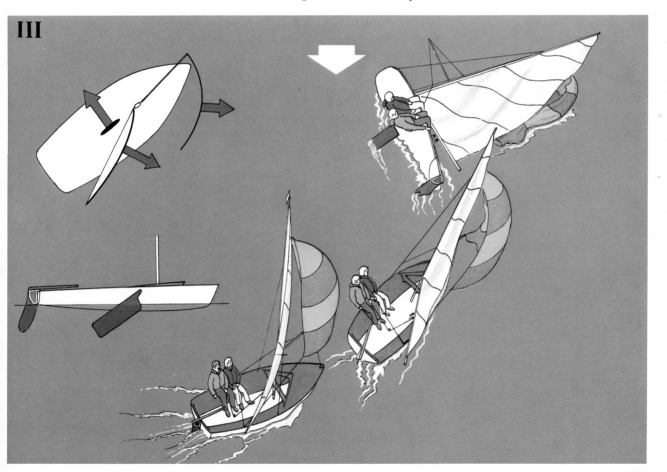

Gybing the spinnaker

On a run:

There can be several variations to these sequences depending on the particular arrangement of the boat but the principles are the same. The main difference is the exact moment that the main boom is gybed. Ideally it should pass the centre line as the spinnaker pole is being thrust out to the new windward side. This has the effect of swinging the spinnaker across the air-stream, helping it to remain full of wind at the moment when it is partially blanketed by the mainsail. It also reaches new clean air-flow soonest.

This can be done easily in a keel boat where the crew can stand in front of the mast but in a dinghy the crew may have to wait until after the mainsail has gone over before taking the pole off the mast and clipping it onto the new tack.

Before the gybe the sheet and guy should be set at the same lengths with the pole at about 45° to the centre line.

Sequences I to VII show a suitable drill.

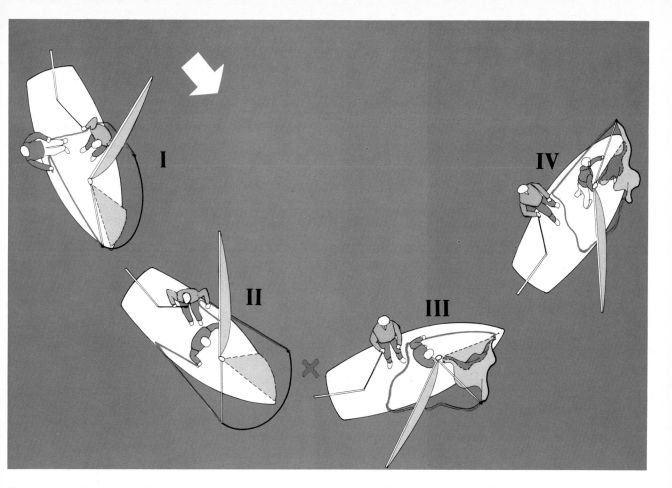

From a reach to a reach:

This is one of the most difficult manoeuvres, especially in a strong wind, and calls for slick team work by helm and crew.

I. The helmsman must bear away smoothly giving the crew time to ease the sheet and set the guy so that the pole is at about 45° to the centre-line. It is a great help if the sheets are marked so that this position can be found easily.

II. With the boat on a run the crew cleats both guy and sheet and makes sure that the guy is not under the reaching hook. Helmsman and crew prepare to gybe the mainsail and jib.

III. Once the main and jib have been gybed and the boat is level the crew moves forward to unclip the pole from the mast and clip it to the new guy. Pushing the outboard end right forwards the crew then unclips the other end from the old guy and clips it to the

mast. The helmsman should be careful not to luff too much or the sail will collapse and the boat may heel uncontrollably.

IV. As soon as the crew has dealt with the pole he can reset the guy for a reach and then sit out and trim the sheet. The helmsman can then steer onto a reach.

Lowering the spinnaker

When it is time to lower the spinnaker, the manoeuvre must be accomplished as quickly as possible and without letting the spinnaker take control. Handling the spinnaker need not be difficult but it is at times that it can flog such as when hoisting, gybing and lowering that troubles usually arise.

The spinnaker is best lowered on a run where the crew and helmsman can stand in the middle of the boat without having to worry about balancing it (1). If it must be lowered on a reach, the helmsman will have to remain sitting out while the crew moves into the boat. The first stage is for the crew to cleat the sheet and guy, or give them to the helmsman (2), while the crew takes the spinnaker pole off the sail and mast and stows

it (3). The crew then pulls in on the guy until he can reach the windward clew (4). While the helmsman eases out the halyard, the crew pulls the spinnaker down by its luff and packs it into its container (5). The crew should pull all of the luff into the bag before trying to pull the foot of the sail in, or it is likely that a twist will develop. While the crew is packing the spinnaker, the helmsman tidies up the sheet and guy (6).

If for some reason it is necessary to lower the spinnaker to leeward—perhaps because the bag for it is on the leeward side—the crew must gather and pack the sail to leeward while the helmsman balances the boat. In a leeward hoist the spinnaker pole can be left on until the sail is lowered. The crew simply grabs the sheet and pulls it in until he holds the clew. Then, while the helmsman lowers the sail,

the crew packs the sail by pulling down on the leech before tidying up the foot. Once the sail is down the pole can be stowed.

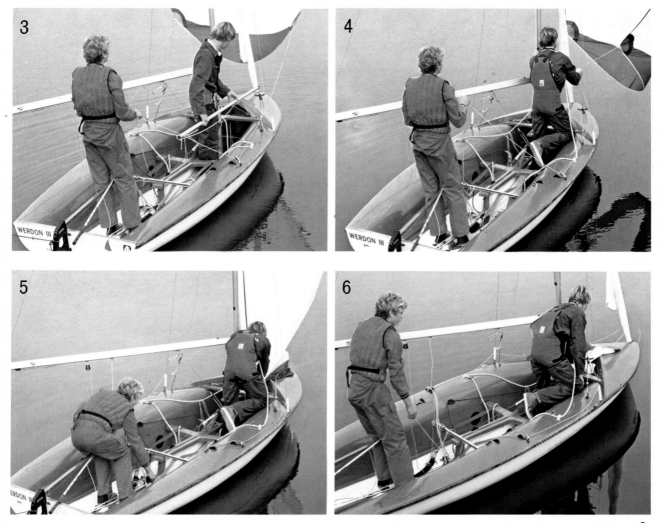

Spinnaker chutes and rollers

Usually spinnakers are stowed and hoisted from containers such as buckets or bags clipped or fitted within the crew's reach somewhere near the mast. There are disadvantages to this system in the length of time that the sail is largely out of proper control.

An improvement is to put the spinnaker under a net on the deck and to pass it out under a roller. It can then be hoisted more directly into position semi-automatically and sets almost immediately.

Even better is to have a **spinnaker chute** which enables the spinnaker to be hoisted directly and also to be lowered and stowed in one operation. The arrangement of the gear is as shown.

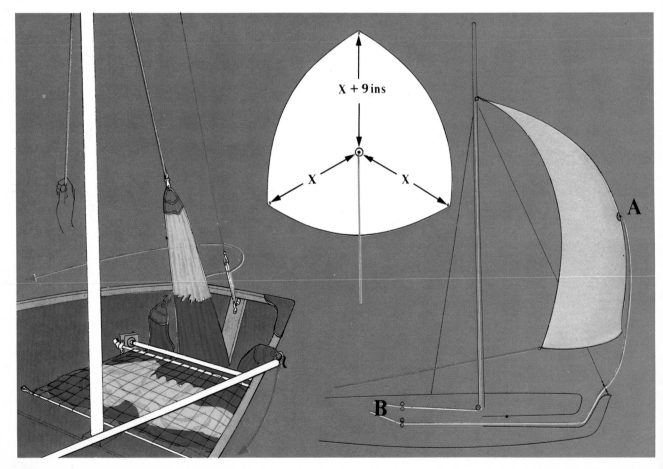

Some dinghies are fitted with a spinnaker chute that makes hoisting and lowering the spinnaker somewhat easier. The sail is stowed in a long tube which has a mouth opening onto the foredeck either just behind or in front of the forestay. The halyard and the sheet and guy are already attached to the sail and all the helmsman has to do to hoist the sail is to pull on the halyard. The sail emerges from the mouth of the chute and the crew can fit the pole in the usual way, although he can help the helmsman by hauling on the guy to get the sail out of the chute more quickly.

Lowering is made possible by a downhaul which is usually the tail of the halyard led through the sock and tube and attached to a patch near the middle of the spinnaker (A). To lower the sail, the sheet and guy are first pulled tight so that the foot of the sail is held against the forestay (E), then the halyard is released and the downhaul pulled (B). The sail will then disappear into the mouth of the chute (C) until finally both clews and the head are inside. As soon as the sail has started to enter the mouth of the chute the crew can release the guy and sheet and remove the pole.

The mouth of the chute is usually made of plastic and should be well rounded and absolutely smooth if friction is to be avoided. The sock inside the boat (D) is normally made from slightly porous material and is also tapered so that air is forced out of the sail as it is lowered. Spinnaker chutes are very useful, but they are also quite hard on sails and many top crews are reverting to normal pouch stowage.

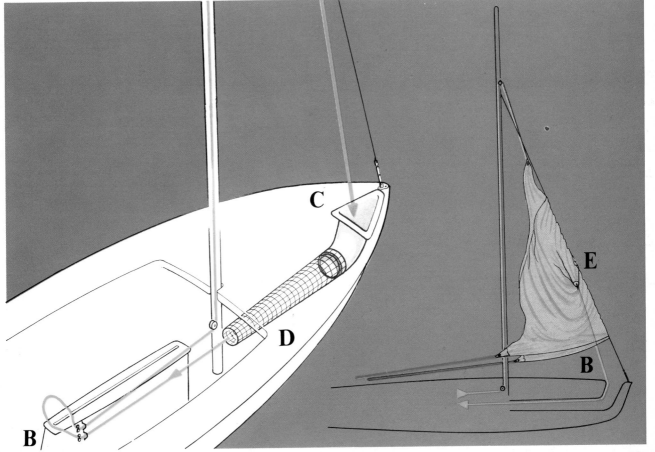

The effect of speed on apparent wind

Apparent wind (w) is the actual wind both in speed and direction that is felt on board. It is the wind which is used by the sails to propel the boat.

Whenever the boat is moving the apparent wind is always to some degree different from the true wind (v).

We have already seen how this affects the boat and crew when sailing to windward compared with running, i.e. more apparent wind speed when close-hauled and less apparent wind speed when running.

Apart from this an understanding of the technicalities of apparent wind is not needed by many sailors, but to get the best out of a boat and especially when planing or using a spinnaker on a light fast dinghy the workings of apparent wind become important.

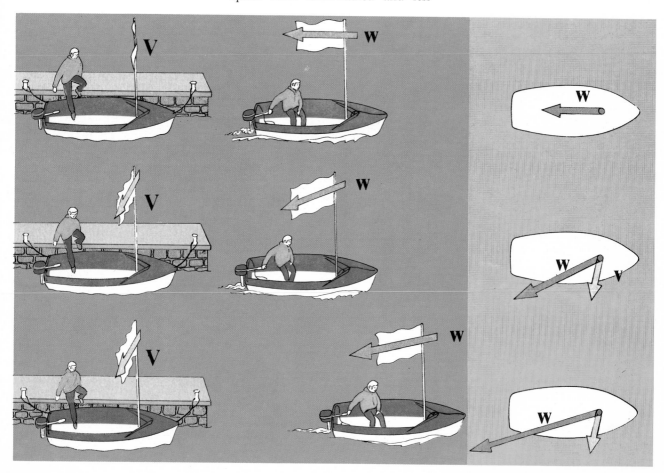

Basically, the faster a boat goes the more the direction of the apparent wind shifts towards coming from ahead.

Secondly, the less the true wind speed the greater is it's shift in direction.

You can if you like draw vector diagrams, formed from arrows proportionate in length to the wind speed, to find out the exact shift in direction and speed in any particular case. But this is of academic interest to the practical sailor who only needs to remember that if the boat accelerates the apparent wind direction will shift to a point more from ahead.

The main occasions when this fact will cause the crew to take some action are when starting to plane, which is described next, and when sailing through waves.

As a boat starts to increase speed by planing the apparent wind comes ahead and so the sheets have to be trimmed in or the boat be borne away. Similarly when accelerating down the face of a wave.

It is usually obvious when it is necessary to sheet in since if this is not done the luffs will shake and the boat will slow down. When the apparent wind shifts aft due to the boat slowing down it is equally vital to adjust the sails but it is not so obvious what has happened since the sails will remain quite full. Unless the sails are eased the boat will slow down because the airflow over the sails will have stalled.

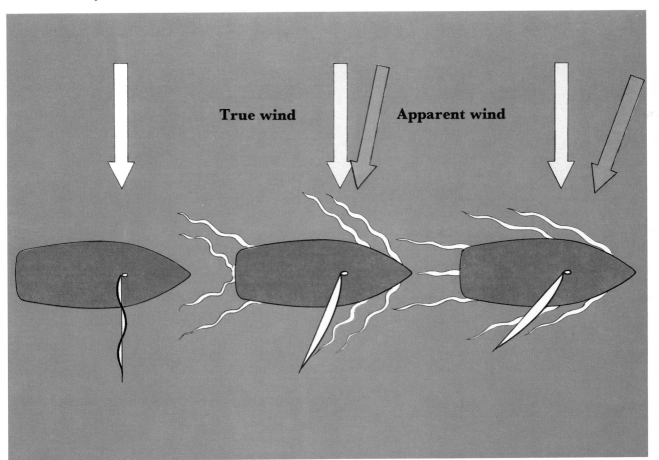

True wind   Apparent wind

The principles of planing

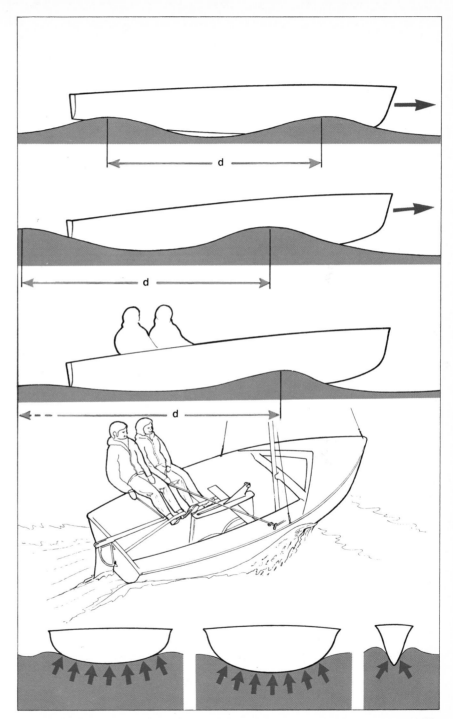

We saw in Part One how the underwater shape of a boat could be designed so that in suitable conditions it would readily start to skim across the water surface rather than cleave through it.

As a boat increases speed it starts to make waves which reduce in number and increase in size (d) until the point is reached where there is one crest supporting the bow and another under the stern with a trough in between. This speed represents the boat's maximum 'displacement speed.' More power produces very little more speed but only causes a bigger pair of waves and a deeper trough.

However, extra power on a light boat can cause it to start climbing up the bow crest and eventually to break through with a sudden burst of increased speed. The sharp bow lifts clear and the flatter midship section is supported by the rushing water. The crew move aft and their weight is supported by the water under the flat stern. The water flow leaves the transom cleanly and without turbulence.

The boat is **planing.**

Planning techniques

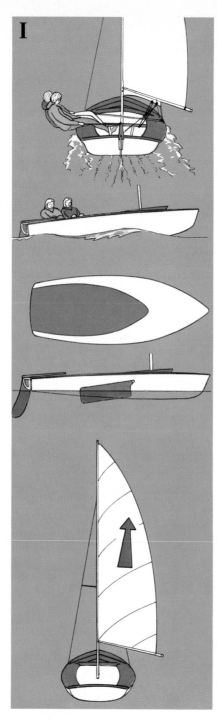

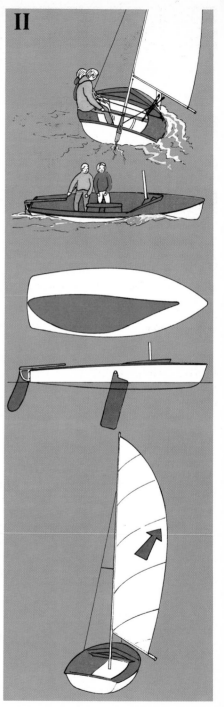

I. Factors which help planing:

Enough wind from a sufficiently favourable direction giving plenty of forward force and a small side force.

Hold the boat level and move crew weight aft to trim the boat so that its designed planing area is in the water.

Reduce resistance by raising the centreboard.

Set the sails for maximum power and tighten the kicking strap to reduce twist.

II. Factors which hinder planing:

Boat heeling and crew too far forward mean that the underwater shape is not suitable and causes too much rudder to be applied.

Centreboard down increases resistance.

Kicking strap slack or mast too flexible takes away power from the sail.

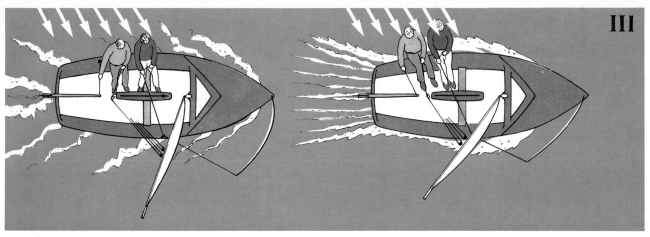

III

Two methods of promoting planing:

III. If the wind is sufficiently far aft all that may be necessary is to wait for a gust and then lean aft, at the same time smartly trimming in both sails together.

As the gust eases gradually edge the boat closer to the wind, trimming in the sails gently. This will give an increase in apparent wind and the boat may remain planing for a little longer.

If a further puff occurs, bear away to reduce heeling and ease the sail slightly.

IV. If the wind is already on the beam and the crew are well outboard an extra gust might be too much for them and cause the boat to heel or spill wind.

This is the moment for them to ease sheets and bear away sharply. The boat will leap into a plane and can then be edged back onto course.

The increased speed makes the boat more stable and often a crew will find that they can edge up closer to the wind after getting planing and while the puff lasts. This is particularly noticeable while planing under spinnaker.

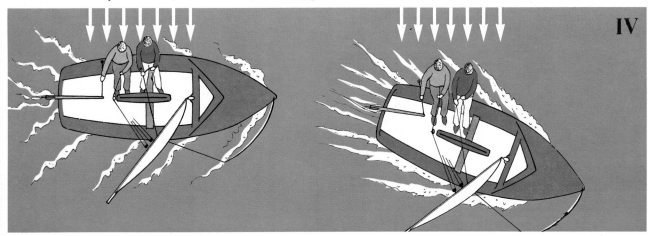

IV

Planing through waves

This can be the most exciting point of sailing. The sense of speed as one sizzles down the face of a wave with spray everywhere is tremendous. And to remain on the wave like a surf-board rider is a thrill which is second to none.

The only real problem is that the boat's course depends on the direction of the waves and this may not be exactly where we want to go. But the speeds and the sensations are of the ultimate in sailing and so it is well worth making a small sacrifice.

The technique of planing through waves and holding position on one is called 'weaving'. As a wave approaches from astern the stern of the boat will lift and there will be an opportunity to gain extra speed from riding the wave.

As the bow drops on the face of the wave every effort should be made to get the boat moving as fast as possible in order to remain on that wave. Shift your body forward slightly to encourage the bow to drop down the face of the wave, sheet in to cope with the apparent wind shifting forward as

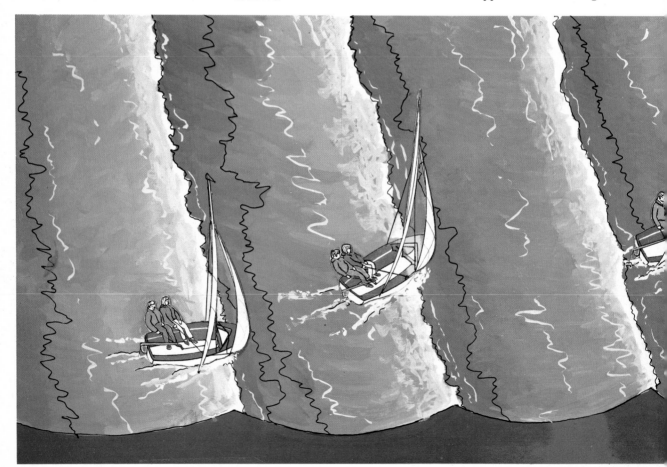

you accelerate, and sit out to keep the boat absolutely level.

As the boat accelerates down the wave move your weight back and luff to retain position on the top face of the wave. If this is not done you will speed off straight down the face and into the trough where you will slow down. The trick now is to hold position on the wave face by luffing and bearing away as necessary. If you bear off too far and find yourself in the trough you must ease out the sails to suit the new apparent wind direction and wait for the crest to overtake you again so that you can try to repeat the performance. Always try to keep the bow of the boat over a hole so that it wants to accelerate downwards but remember to luff back onto the wave face before you hit the bottom! Watch surfers playing with waves and you will see the same actions being performed. If you lose a wave, immediately adjust the sails for the new wind direction and watch for the next big wave crest to approach. It is often a surprise to sailors experiencing surfing for the first time to realise the extra speed available from riding big waves. When they catch a wave they are taken by surprise and forget to sheet in as the apparent wind shifts forwards. Of course their sails shake and they lose the wave. In fact the apparent wind can shift so far forwards that it is often possible, even when on a run, to bear away across the wave face rather than luffing in order to stay on the wave and head in the right direction.

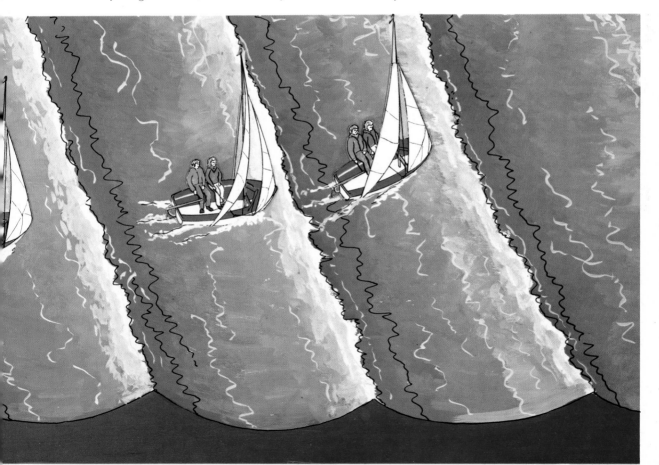

The principles of adjusting the rig

As was briefly mentioned in Part One, there are various ways of adjusting the shape and flow of the sails around the mean basic shape for which the sail was designed.

Some of these adjustments are made by putting more or less tension on various control points such as the clew outhaul, the sliding gooseneck, the halyard, the cunningham tackle at the tack, the kicking strap and of course the sheet.

Other adjustments can be made to operate automatically to some degree. For example, a gust of wind can cause the mast to bend a little extra and this can be arranged to take power out of the sail.

The first basic requirement is to flatten the section of the sail, thus reducing its power output for sailing in hard winds.

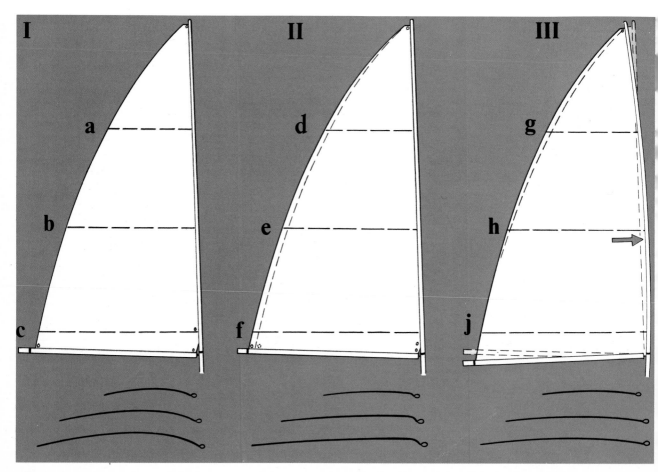

I. A sail set on straight spars and with just enough tension on the luff and foot to remove wrinkles will be ideal for light winds and have typical flow sections as in a, b and c.

II. Putting tension on the clew out-haul and the cunningham tackle puts heavy creases at the luff and foot which are blown out smooth by the wind. The point of maximum flow moves right forward and the leach area is flattened; d, e, f.

III. If the mast is now bent by some means the pocket near the luff can be removed to a greater or lesser extent thus flattening the flow over the whole sail; g, h, j.

IV. Mast bend in the plane of the sail is accomplished when close-hauled by sheeting in. This puts tension on the leach which pulls the mast top aft. This force is also trans-mitted to the gooseneck pushing the mast forward.

V. On a reach, the kicking strap does the same job of mast bending and also limits sail twist. Too much twist and only part of the sail can accept the wind and allow smooth air-flow. The rest will either be stalled or be lifting and so produce less power and at an incorrect angle; k, l, m. All parts of an untwisted sail will have smooth air-flow; n.

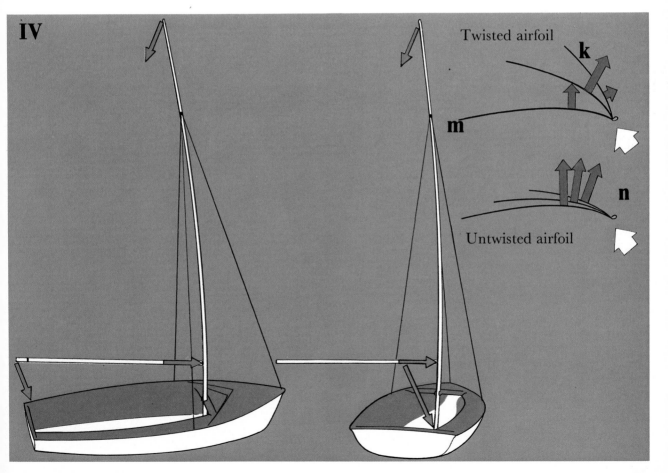

The effects of side bend

The flexing of the mast sideways can be the most useful means of automatically adjusting the mainsail to the effects of a gust or a lull.

The kicking strap and mainsheet are assumed to be fixed and only control fore and aft bend. It is the basic flexibility of the mast, often aided by spreaders and other devices, which governs the amount and the limit of sideways bend.

Extra wind pressure causes the leach area, especially high up, to drop off to leeward. This is limited by the springing effect of the mast. The result is to twist the sail and to flatten the upper part.

Power is reduced especially high up where the heeling moment is greatest. When the gust passes or when a lull appears, the mast returns upright and draws the leach to windward again. The flow in the sail section is increased and power is restored.

Adjusting air-flow across the jib

I. The flow in the jib cannot be adjusted so comprehensively as in the mainsail. Its luff is set on a wire which more often than not bends the wrong way thus introducing extra flow when the opposite is required. Hence a tight forestay is needed when close-hauled.

Some jibs however have loose luffs and they can be pre-tensioned like the mainsail with a cunningham tackle at the tack.

II. The jib fairlead position is the other main control. If placed too far forward the leach will be too tight throwing too much curve into the upper part of the sail and thus deflecting turbulent air into the mainsail. The foot will be slack and will flap.

III. If placed too far aft the foot will be drawn tight and the leach will drop off to leeward and flap. If not done to excess this is a useful technique for reducing power in hard winds.

The same effects as in II and III can be obtained by raking the mast more upright (II) or more aft (III) or by raising the tack of the jib (II) or lowering it (III).

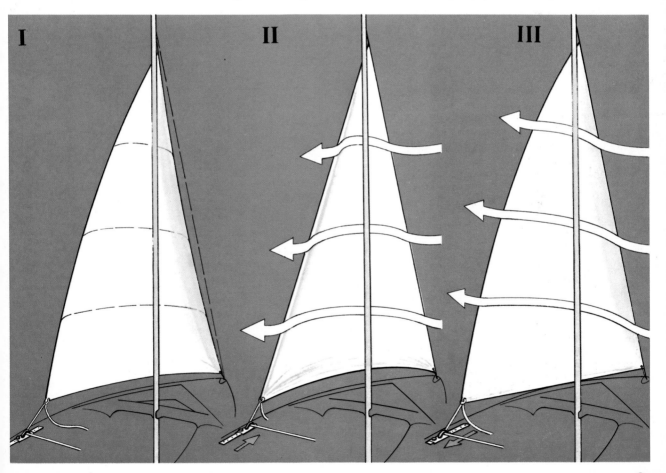

Controlling mast bend—fore and aft

I. When sailing closed-hauled the tendency is for the mast to bend, caused firstly by leach tension acting on the mast top and secondly by the boom thrust at the gooseneck. But once a bend has been started it is increased by compression in the mast mainly in the area between the hounds and the heel.

II. The jib needs a tight straight forestay for it to set well close-hauled though the sailmaker can allow for a limited amount of sag.

III. When the mast bends the distance between the hounds and the heel is shortened and the forestay sags. Maintaining tension on the mainsheet will however tighten it at the expense of a little extra mast rake and a slackening of the lee shroud. The former can be of slight automatic help in slackening the leach of the jib in a gust.

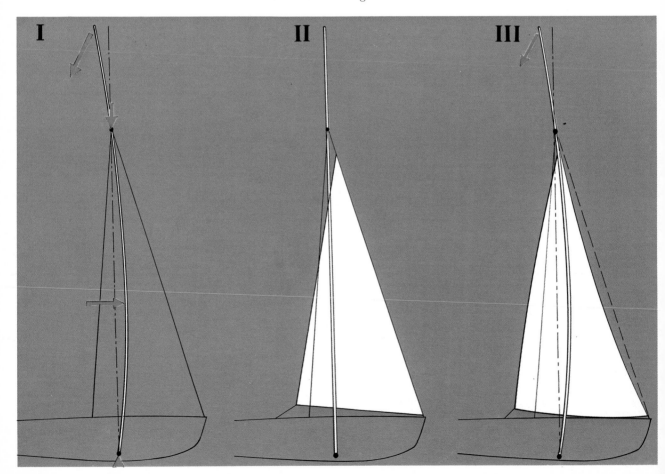

IV. One method of limiting fore and aft bend is to have a variable stop in front of the mast at the mast gate. This can be in the form of chocks of various thicknesses or a more sophisticated screw or lever jack.

V. Additional support is usually provided by spreaders which can be either free swinging, limited swinging or fixed. Spreaders are connected at their outer ends to the shrouds and to a bracket on the mast at their inboard ends. Free-swinging spreaders only provide sideways support and suffer the disadvantage that the middle of the mast can move back under pressure from a spinnaker which can cause the mast to collapse.

VI. The limited-swing spreader is the most commonly used. It provides fore-and-aft and athwartships support but the lee spreader can move forward to allow the mainsail to be fully eased off-wind.

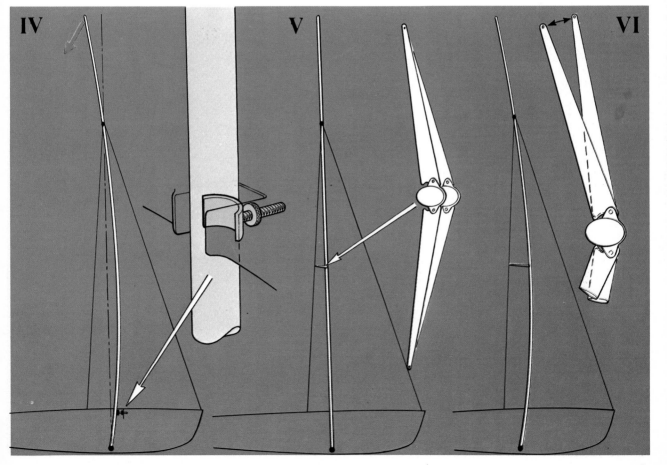

Controlling mast bend— sideways

I. Starting with a mast held at the heel and hounds only, the forces affecting side bend are almost entirely confined to the mast top.

II. There is no boom pressure acting sideways but, due to the angle of the sail to the centreline, the side of the mast gate can limit to some extent both side bend when close-hauled and also bend in the plane of the sail when reaching.

III. Side bend can be better controlled by spreaders and **diamond bracing** (A) but in the case of spreaders connected to the shroud it is usually only the windward shroud which is effective because this is the only one under tension.

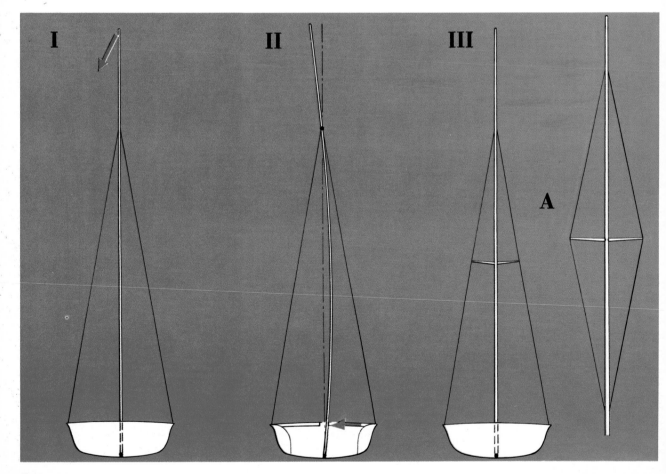

Controlling multiple forces

IV. The forces on a mast are not often simple. More usually a combination of fore and aft, sideways and compression strains have to be controlled. In addition there is twist.

Spreaders can be made longer or shorter. Long spreaders which deflect the shroud outboard will push the middle of the mast to leeward and so reduce sideways bend. Short spreaders which pull the shroud in towards the mast will tend to pull the middle of the mast to windward and so increase sideways bend.

V. Pure sideways movement is resisted only by the windward shroud, the lee one being almost always slack.

VI. When forward bend takes place the mast centre moves forward until the spreaders come up against their stops (B) and then the whole mast tries to twist (C), pivoting about outer end of the windward spreader. The lee shroud, being slack, does nothing to prevent this and the result is excessive mast bend.

The only way of controlling this twist and bend is to clamp the mast heel rigidly in its step (D) so that it cannot turn (E).

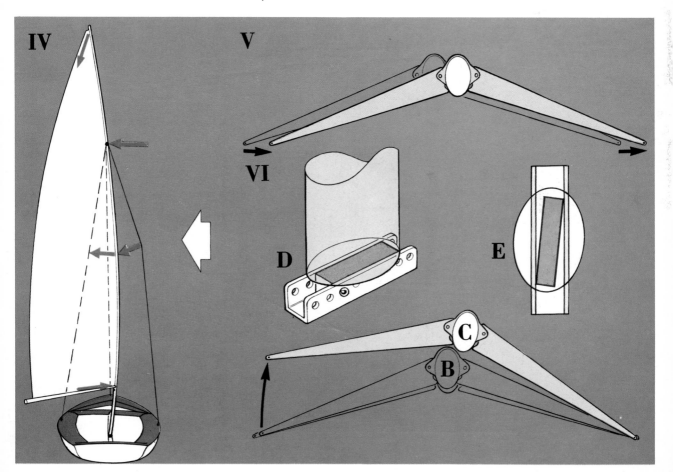

Hard weather techniques

In blowing weather, steps should be taken to reduce wind resistance, increase righting power and improve the sail's driving angle.

A. Flatten the flow in the sail by extra tension on clew outhaul.

B. Flatten leach area and move position of maximum flow forward by tensioning cunningham tackle.

C. Take twist out of the sail, promote mast bend and reduce wind resistance by tensioning the kicking strap.

D. Ease off jib leach by moving fairlead aft.

E. Get crew weight further outboard to increase righting lever.

F. Keep crew together to reduce wind resistance.

G. Move traveller outboard when close hauled to improve angle of driving force and partially raise centreboard to improve balance.

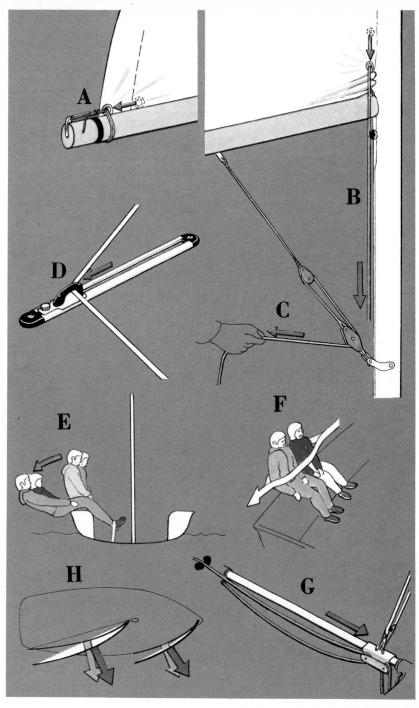

Reefing and shortening sail

If wind and sea conditions are so severe that full sail still produces too much power even after all normal steps have been taken, then some sail area will have to be taken away (A).

Reducing sail area temporarily by rolling or furling a part of it is called **reefing.** 'Shortening sail' is the same or, more usually, substituting a smaller sail or taking one sail off altogether.

The normal arrangements on a light dinghy are to roll part of the foot of the sail round the boom. The gooseneck is specially made to do this with a squared shank (B).

Partially remove the boom from the gooseneck, roll the boom whilst easing the halyard making sure that the luff rope beds down smoothly and tight. Reinsert the gooseneck and tension the halyard (C).

A helper should pull on the leach to prevent wrinkles being rolled in (D).

Mainsails with blocks hung

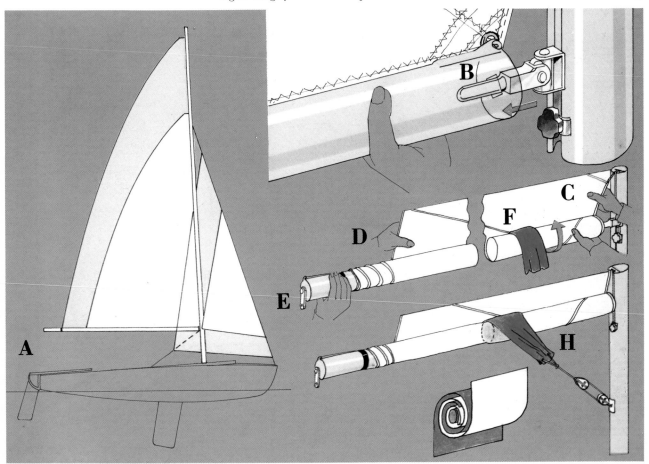

from a swivel tang on the boom end can be reefed without difficulty (E).

Centre-mainsheet boats, however, have a problem with rolling the sail around the boom and this is not usually done unless the centre-mainsheet blocks are fitted on a claw-ring. The kicking strap must, of course, be removed when rolling the sail around the boom unless it is fitted to a claw-ring, but a good replacement can be arranged by rolling the sail bag in with the sail (F). The kicking strap tackle is then attached to the draw-string at the top of the bag (H) which should be just protruding from the rolled up sail. On older boats the points method of reefing is still sometimes used and when it can be used results in a well-setting reefed sail (I). (L) shows an alternative.

The sail is first lashed down at the reefed tack cringle and the reefed clew cringle (J) and then the surplus cloth (G) is bunched and tied at the reef points by crossing the lines under the sail and then round the boom, tying them underneath with a reef knot (K). Jibs are rarely reefed but can be changed for a smaller one.

In an emergency the area of a jib can be reduced by rolling it around the forestay for a few turns.

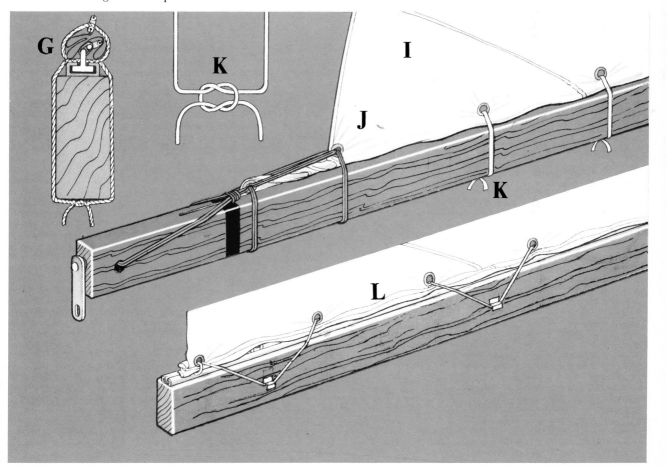

Sailing reefed and with one sail

Reefing or shortening sail alters the balance of the boat. A comparison of the two drawings shows why the dynamic centre of effort (DCE) of the sails tends to move forward when reefed. The centre of lateral resistance (CLR) stays the same. The new forward position of the DCE means that the bow is pushed to leeward, the boat pivoting around the CLR. The boat is said to be carrying **lee helm** and this is disconcerting to the helmsman. It can also be dangerous since the boat may bear away uncontrollably in a gust. The opposite to lee helm is **weather helm** and a very small degree is desirable for safety.

It is important that the boat's balance is not too much affected and so if the mainsail is to be reefed more than a little, a smaller jib should be set to restore balance (a).

Alternatively, take the jib off altogether and correct the resulting excessive weather helm by swinging the centreboard aft (b).

Lifting the centreboard a little improves steering in hard winds even

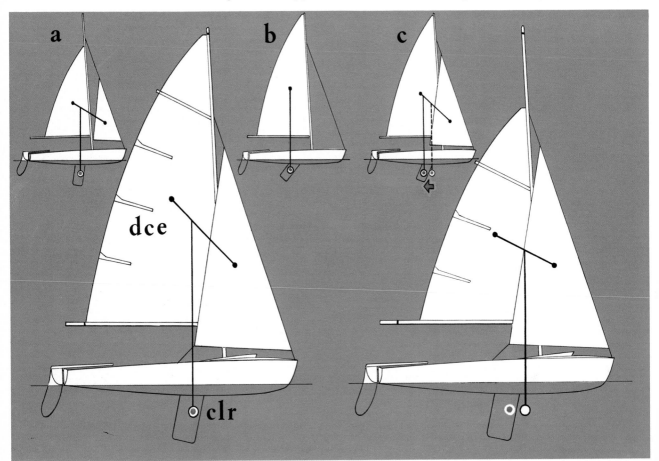

a   b   c

dce

clr

under full sail (c) because weather helm increases with the wind and can become excessive.

Often the boat is under better control under a properly set full mainsail alone than under a reefed mainsail and jib.

It is important to remember when sailing close-hauled in hard winds that the wind resistance of the boat will be higher. If at the same time the sails are flattened and the mast bent to reduce sail power, or the sails are reefed for the same purpose, then it can readily be understood that the lower forward force may not be able to overcome the higher drag when close hauled (d).

Speed must be kept up in hard winds because accurate steering is essential to correct trim in sudden gusts and to avoid hitting waves head-on which also add to the forward resistance.

Therefore, in these conditions do not try to sail very close to the wind. Let the traveller out, ease sheets and get the boat moving fast. Overall windward progress will be better and the boat will be under safer control.

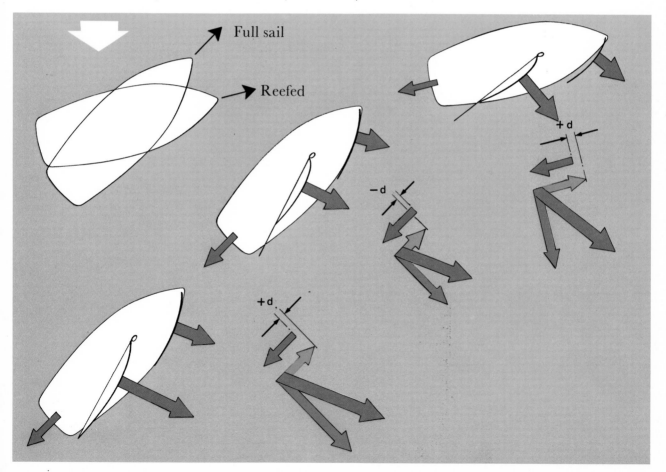

Heaving-to

When a boat **heaves-to** it is lying stopped for an appreciable but temporary period but not anchored or moored.

The easiest way of stopping is to let go the sheets and allow the sails to flap free. However this is not very desirable for more than a very brief period since the sails suffer excessive wear when flapping and it is not restful to have to listen to them banging and slatting.

The best way to heave-to in a dinghy is to sheet the jib in on the windward side (known as 'backing the jib'), raise the centreboard two-thirds, put the tiller hard a-lee and then sheet in the mainsail just sufficiently to maintain a steady heading slightly closer than beam-on to the wind.

The boat will lie comparatively quietly and drift to leeward and forwards slowly, but with a light dinghy you will have to keep a steadying hand on the tiller.

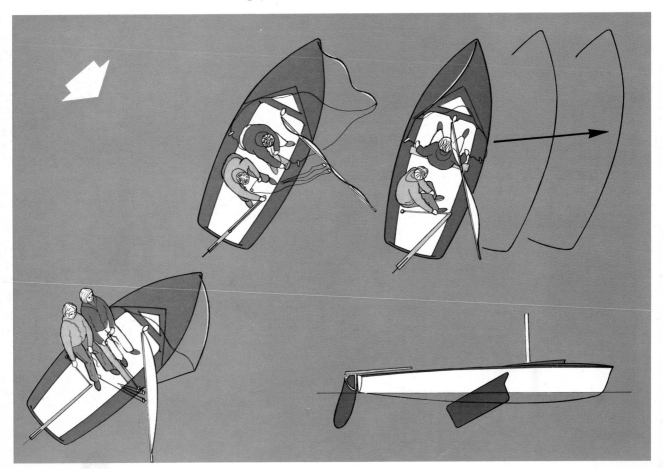

Man overboard

Some of the techniques were explained in Part Two. One has to remember that a light dinghy should not be allowed to get too far to leeward of the swimming man because the crew remaining on board may not have enough weight and strength to drive the boat back to windward against a fresh wind and waves.

I. So, the moment you realize your companion is in the water, put the boat beam on to the wind with sails flapping until you have decided what to do.

If you can manage both the mainsail and the jib you should sail away on a reach and then tack. Allow yourself sufficient room to manoeuvre and to aim the boat properly to come close to leeward of the swimmer and to luff and stop alongside. Bring the swimmer aboard over the windward side (A).

II. If it is blowing hard, lower and lash the jib, half raise the centreboard (B) to correct balance and then continue as before.

For the reasons explained in Part III, page 135, you should bring a light dinghy to leeward of the swimmer.

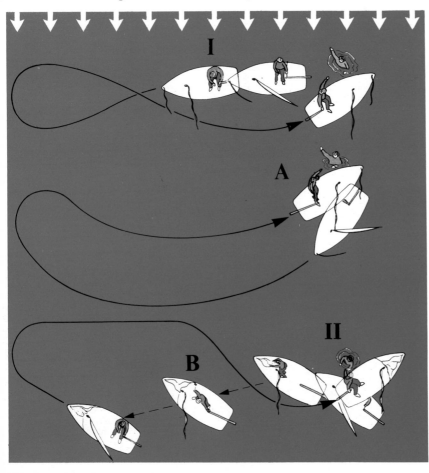

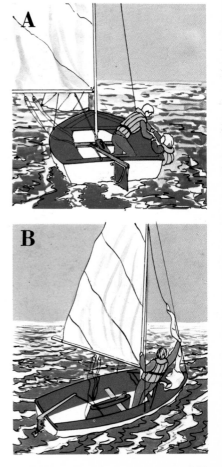

The distribution of emergency buoyancy

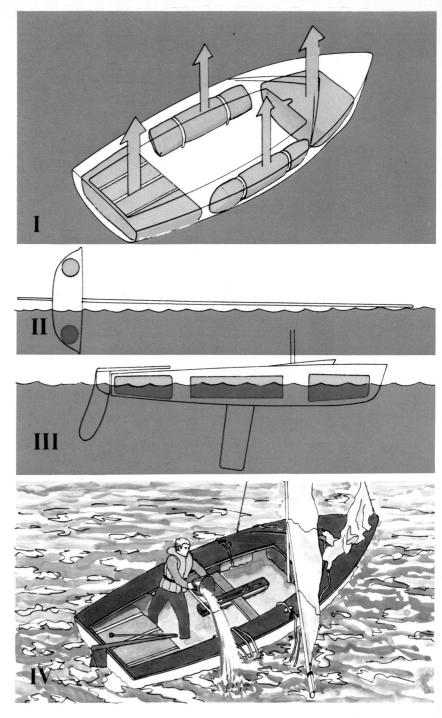

I. Ideally a boat should have plenty of surplus emergency floatation in the bow and stern with a comparatively small amount on each side.

II. Ideally also the capsized hull should float on its own with the centreboard only just clear of the water and the mast lying nearly flat.

III. Distribution of the floatation tanks as shown will float the flooded hull in a stable manner with the gunwale a few inches clear all round.

IV. The crew can move about safely, bail out the water and lower sails if required.

Many dinghies do not have this ideal arrangement of tanks or bags. Crews should be aware of the problems resulting from variations from this ideal and be prepared to deal with them.

V. Too little buoyancy is almost impossible to manage and the crew should hang on and await help. The hull will be unstable and tend to turn over in the water **VI**. Often it will finally end up with the bow in the air and be extremely difficult to grasp.

VII. Too much buoyancy can be almost as dangerous. Because the hull floats so high, the mast tends to sink and the boat rapidly finishes bottom up and is then difficult to hang on to and to right.

If it does not turn upside down it can still be impossible to right because the vital centreboard will be out of reach.

VIII. Finally there is the danger of becoming separated from the boat when it blows downwind faster than the crew can swim, thus inadvertantly breaking the one 'Golden Rule'—*Always stay with your boat.*

How capsizes occur

Knowing how the more common capsizes can happen may help to avoid them.

I. Simple over-powering is caused by strong wind, loss of control due to too little speed and not enough crew weight. The boom end dragging in the water is the final cause.

II. Broken gear is a frequent cause and results from poor maintenance or the use of fittings of the wrong type. Broken toe-straps are often the culprits.

Windward capsizes are more difficult to recover from since the crew will find themselves with the boat on top of them and then have to swim around to the other side which wastes time.

III. Letting go the tiller or the mainsheet, a sudden lull in the wind, or a heading shift in the wind when close-hauled can all cause a windward capsize.

IV. Bearing away too suddenly or letting the mainsail out too far on a run frequently causes a very sudden capsize which often throws the crew some way from the boat and is perhaps the most potentially dangerous.

. A broach under spinnaker caused by excessive heel and too much power, or by having the centreboard down too far can cause a leeward capsize.

V. A broach to windward or to leeward caused by a gust, incorrect spinnaker trim, or too much or too little centreboard, can cause a capsize either way!

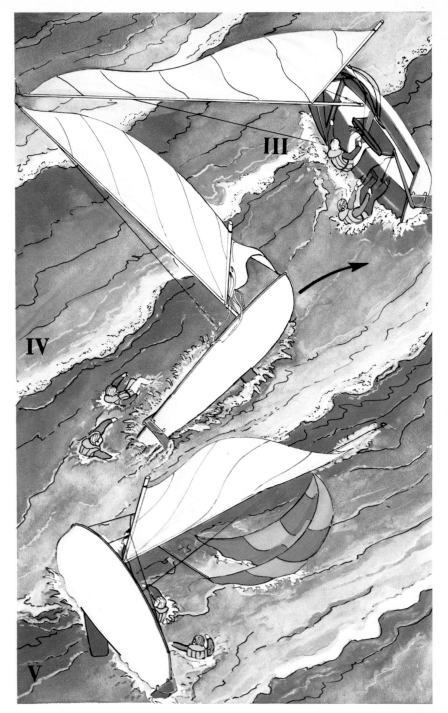

Righting the boat

All boats react in different ways when capsized—some float very high on their sides, some invert immediately and some lie quietly waiting to be righted. No one method can work all the time but the one described here is effective on most occasions.

When the boat capsizes one crew member (the heaviest) should make his way around the boat to the centreboard and climb on to it. The other person should lie in the water next to the boat and alongside the thwart or centreboard case (**V**). The person on the centreboard then grasps the jib sheet, leans back and attempts to right the boat. As the boat comes upright the sidedeck that is under water will come up under the person

lying inside the boat and he will be scooped inside (**VI**). With the boat upright and one man already inside the person righting the boat can climb in or be helped into the boat by his partner (**VII**). As soon as the boat is upright it should be bailed dry in order to avoid the instability caused by loose water slopping around inside as the boat heels (**VIII**).

I–IV show a continental method used to prevent the boat inverting in shallow and smooth water. The crew swims to the masthead after working free of the boat and keeps it level while the other crew member climbs on the centreboard. When there is weight on the centreboard, the crew at the masthead has to make his way back to the hull and the righting proceeds as

before. This method is unsound because of the difficulty of reaching the masthead. Waves passing under the boat and mast could easily cause the person at the masthead to lose his grip and become separated from the boat.

III

IV

VII

VIII

A common problem

I. The crew have correctly done the first part of the routine after a leeward capsize except that both crew have climbed onto the centreboard, or one of them is still in the water but away from the boat.

II. A dinghy with a large surplus of buoyancy will offer a great deal of wind resistance when lying on its side and the hull will very quickly start to blow round to leeward. In position II it is already too late for the crew to try to right the boat by the standard method.

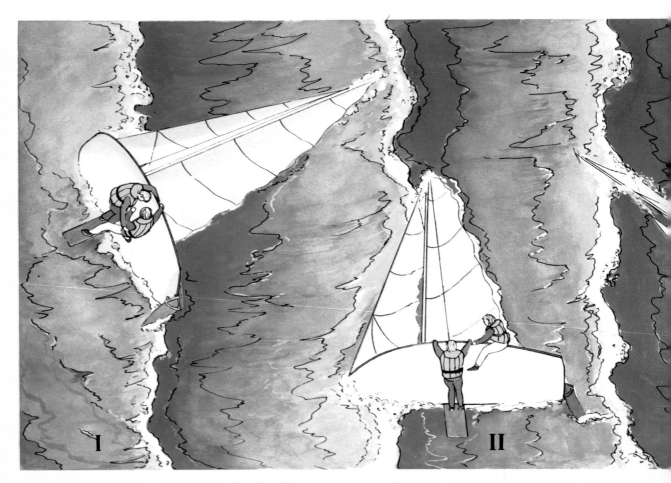

I

II

III. It is astonishing how many times we see crews trying to right the boat from this position with the hull lying to leeward of the rig.

IV. The wind gets under the sail and lifts the mast up very suddenly and far too fast for the crew to climb in over the side. Their weight is now on the lee side . . .

V. . . . and the boat simply capsizes again on top of them. After one or two attempts at this the crew will be getting very tired and cold.

The whole secret of successful righting is to know what will happen and to take the correct action fast. If the boat does tend to blow round to leeward of the rig it is often worthwhile having the crew hold the bow of the boat. His body will act as a sea-anchor and help hold the boat head to wind while it is righted.

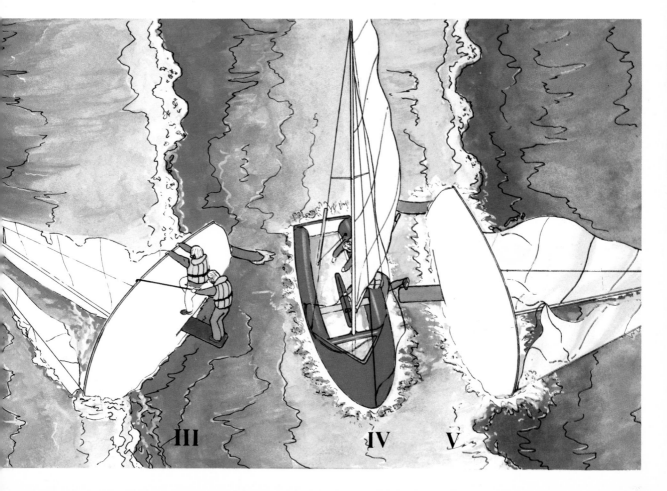

III   IV   V

More problems

If the boat has turned upside down one can climb on board via the rudder which should have been prevented from falling off by its clip. Take hold of the centreboard and stand with the wind at your back with your feet on the lip between hull and deck. Lean back and be prepared to wait, for the boat will come up very slowly at first. It can help for the other member of the crew to press down on one of the aft corners to break the suction that forms between the water and the deck (I).

Alternatively the second crew member can grasp the other round the waist to help pull the boat up to the horizontal. If the centreboard has dropped back into its slot, use a jib sheet led over the hull to pull the boat up to horizontal when the crew can then lower the board again (II and III).

With the boat now lying on its side (IV), sort out any gear that may have fallen out when it was upside down but do not leave the boat to swim after any gear that was not tied on and has floated away. Proceed to right the boat in the way that has already been described (V and VI).

If you suspect that the mast is stuck in the bottom do not climb onto the boat since your weight will help drive it in further. Instead pass the jib sheet over the hull and, lying in the water with your feet against the edge of the deck, try and rotate the boat onto its side. If you find that after several attempts you still cannot right the boat, try and attract attention, climb up onto the boat and tie yourself to it.

Motor boat assistance

A capsize under spinnaker can cause a lot of problems because as soon as the spinnaker hits the water it tries to tangle around every part of the boat imaginable. It is vital to try to prevent the boat from inverting so one person should attempt to get onto the centreboard as fast as possible. If both of the crew are quick they can both land on the board and right the boat almost immediately and before a tangle has resulted. Otherwise it is worth considering lowering the spin-

naker since it can be very difficult to right a dinghy with the spinnaker attempting to capsize it again immediately. If it is decided to right the boat with the spinnaker still up it will probably need both of the crew on the board. In this case at least one of them should be ready to dive into the boat as it comes up to balance it and help the other one in. As soon as possible after righting the boat sort out all the gear, which may mean lowering the spinnaker before sailing off.

On some occasions you may need outside assistance in order to right the boat and get it home. You should always be careful, however, of accepting help from someone you do not know since it is very easy for a bad rescue boat skipper to quickly wreck your boat. Sometimes the rescue boat can help simply by taking your painter and motoring very slowly into the wind while you right the boat and sort yourselves out. On other occasions he will have to provide more help. The 'Golden Rule' for the helmsman of the rescue boat is always to go for the masthead. Once he has hold of the mast he should work his way down the forestay with the rigging on top of the rescue boat. As he approaches the hull he can lift up on the forestay and the boat will come upright and hang head to wind from the rescue boat if the centreboard is raised. The rescue boat can then hold your boat head to wind while you sort out yourselves and the boat.

The principle of the trapeze

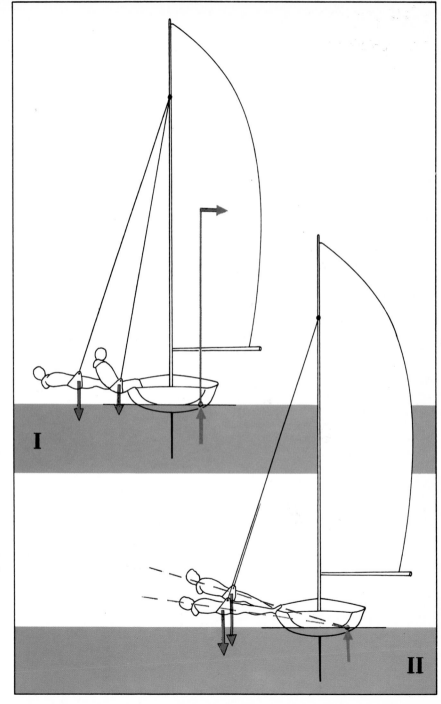

The **trapeze** was developed for racing boats. It enables the same crew in the same boat to carry more sail area or more powerful sails with any given wind speed.

I. The principle is to get some of the crew's weight further outboard thus increasing their total righting moment.

The extra capacity to carry sail means increased power and greater speed. In fact some light dinghies can be made to plane when sailing very nearly close-hauled if one of the crew is on a trapeze.

II. The trapeze is essentially a harness round the body, clipped to a wire led from the hounds. The length of the wire is important since the more horizontal the crew, the greater the righting lever.

Preparing the trapeze

The drawings show a typical arrangement of trapeze gear.

Points to note:
The trapeze wires are made from finer wire than the shrouds. The trapeze wire is attached to a grab handle which should be just within a straight arm reach of the trapezing crew.

A block is attached to the handle through which runs a line connected at one end to the trapeze ring. The other end has an adjustable stop to bring the ring to the correct height. The line is also attached to a length of shockcord which runs in front of the mast to the trapeze gear on the other side of the boat. The two positions on the trapeze ring allow the crew to adjust his height. Some arrangements incorporate an adjustable tackle for further height adjustment.

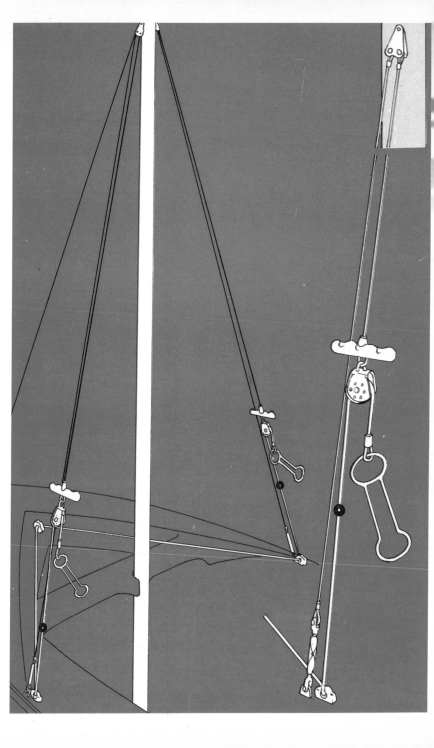

The harness is very important since it must be comfortable and have the right features. It is worth getting the best type available.

Important features:
Strong, stiff and well padded seat and waist-band wide enough to spread the strain over a large area.
Adjustable shoulder straps and crutch strap to hold the waist-band securely from slipping up or down.
Adjustable waist straps to hold the hook close to the body.
All loose ends of straps held down by Velcro strip fasteners.
Very strong hook plate with rubber preventer to stop the ring falling out.

I. The harness should be positioned so that the hook is only just above the body's centre of gravity. If not, it will be very tiring to remain straight and fully out. Also it will be impossible to swing inboard, neither can the wire ever be of the most effective length.

II. When trapezing the hook plate must be close to the body and the grab-handle should be within easy reach.

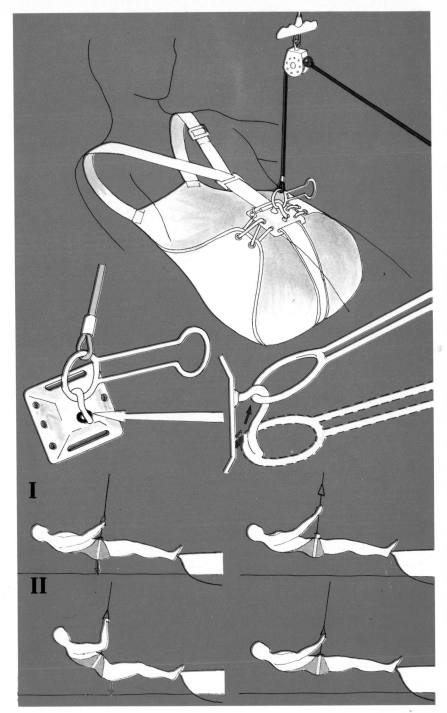

209

Hooking on and pushing out

Trapezing is one of the best experiences available to the dinghy sailor. There is nothing quite like skimming low over the water on a trapeze supported only by a thin wire.

Trapezing is not difficult and is, in fact, much less tiring than sitting out, but it does need a bit of practice if you are not to annoy your helmsman with clumsy footwork.

I. Sit on the sidedeck and clip the ring into your harness hook with your front hand.

II. Drop your backside over the edge of the deck so that all your weight is taken on the trapeze wire. Bend your front leg at the knee and place your foot on the deck edge.

III. Keeping the jib sheet in your aft hand push out with your front foot and bring your other foot onto the deck edge.

IV. Straighten your legs, let go the handle and you are trapezing. Don't keep your feet together or you will find that it is difficult to keep your balance, especially if the boat hits a wave and slows down. Swinging around the forestay is undignified!

V. To come back in, all you have to do is bend your legs and repeat the procedure in reverse. Make sure that your front foot comes in aft of the shroud or you will find yourself unable to move. When you are trapezing don't forget that you still have your other duties as crew—you must trim the jib and keep an eye out for other boats. In fact the jib sheet can provide a bit of security for you in your first

few attempts since it will help you to keep your balance against the forward pull of the trapeze wire. The other way of preventing the wire from pulling you forward is to keep your front foot straight but your aft one slightly bent.

Trapezing techniques

Just learning to stay out on the trapeze is only the beginning of getting the best out of the equipment and keeping your helmsman happy. Remember that in a trapeze dinghy the crew is every bit as important as the helmsman and can have a very important effect on the boat by his movements on the wire. Always aim to trapeze as low as possible. Ideally you should be horizontal when the boat is upright since then you will be exerting the maximum amount of leverage. In practice, though, you will often have to raise yourself up slightly in order to avoid hitting waves or to make it easier to play the spinnaker.

Have the trapeze adjusted to suit yourself. A good guide, especially for the beginner, is to adjust the tackle so that you can just hook onto the upper ring when you are sitting on the sidedeck next to the shroud. Always make sure that your trapeze harness fits you snugly with the hook close to your midriff, which in most people approximates to their centre of gravity. If the belt is too high it will be hard work standing out on the wire and if it is too low you may find that your feet disappear up in the air as you overbalance backwards. Once you have got used to lying out on the wire practise moving backwards and forwards along the gunwale. The expert trapeze hand will be able to move through quite a distance and can thus affect the trim of the boat quite considerably. Always remember to resist the forwards pull of the wire by keeping the front leg straight and the back one slightly bent.

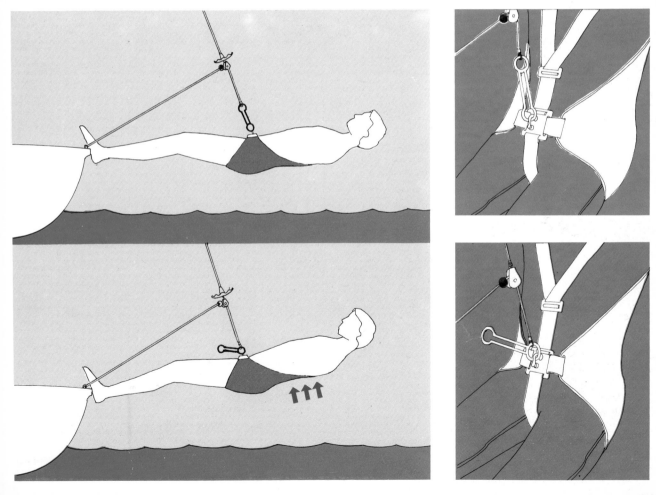

Trapezing

It is not difficult to trapeze in flat water and steady winds of Force 3 or above (1). The difficulty arises when the wind is shifty or changeable in strength and when sailing in waves. When the wind is changeable the trapezing crew will have to be constantly alert to move his weight to keep the boat level (2). Providing the crew has confidence in the helmsman and vice versa, they have a righting power and facility for adjusting trim and balance that is varied and comprehensive. A good crew is light and lively on his feet and can swing in and out as necessary.

When the helmsman bears away to weave through waves the crew can ease the jib sheet by bending his legs (3), straightening them again to snap the jib sheet in and to exert more righting power as the helmsman luffs (4). When planing, the crew must move backwards and forwards on the gunwale to adjust the boat's trim. In these conditions a footstrap on the gunwale by the helmsman is useful and prevents the crew being thrown forwards (5).

The crew should always try to keep right alongside the helmsman so that their wind resistance is as little as possible and should also keep low to avoid blocking the helmsman's view (6).

The helmsman should remember that his actions can have a pronounced effect on the trapeze hand (7). For instance, if he bears away too violently the crew may find his feet leaving the gunwale as centrifugal force whips him away from the boat. Always give your crew ample warning of any manoeuvre you plan to make and make sure they can hear you; it is sometimes difficult to hear your helmsman from the end of the trapeze wire!